PENGUIN BOOKS

AN EXALTATION OF LARKS

James Lipton is an author, playwright, lyricist, director, choreographer, and producer. The son of a prominent American poet, he was himself a published poet by the age of twelve. He is the author of the novel *Mirrors*, for the film version of which he was a screenwriter and producer. In the past five years, Mr. Lipton has written eight motion pictures, and in the past twenty has written and produced hundreds of hours of award-winning television drama and entertainment specials. He has written the book and lyrics of two Broadway musicals, and was recently nominated for a television Emmy for his lyrics. This greatly expanded ultimate edition of *An Exaltation of Larks* is Mr. Lipton's delighted celebration of a twenty-two-year span during which the acclaimed book, which he calls his letter to the world, has never been out of print.

An
Exaltation
of
Larks

The Ultimate Edition

James Lipton

PENGUIN BOOKS

PENGUIN BOOKS
Published by the Penguin Group
Penguin Group (USA) Inc., 375 Hudson Street, New York, New York 10014, U.S.A.
Penguin Group (Canada), 90 Eglinton Avenue East, Suite 700, Toronto,
Ontario, Canada M4P 2Y3 (a division of Pearson Penguin Canada Inc.)
Penguin Books Ltd, 80 Strand, London WC2R 0RL, England
Penguin Ireland, 25 St Stephen's Green, Dublin 2, Ireland (a division of Penguin Books Ltd)
Penguin Group (Australia), 250 Camberwell Road, Camberwell,
Victoria 3124, Australia (a division of Pearson Australia Group Pty Ltd)
Penguin Books India Pvt Ltd, 11 Community Centre, Panchsheel Park, New Delhi – 110 017, India
Penguin Group (NZ), cnr Airborne and Rosedale Roads,
Albany, Auckland 1310, New Zealand (a division of Pearson New Zealand Ltd)
Penguin Books (South Africa) (Pty) Ltd, 24 Sturdee Avenue,
Rosebank, Johannesburg 2196, South Africa

Penguin Books Ltd, Registered Offices: 80 Strand, London WC2R 0RL, England

First published in the United States of America
by Grossman Publishers 1968
Second edition published in Penguin Books 1977
Third edition published by Viking Penguin,
a division of Penguin Books USA Inc., 1991
Published in Penguin Books 1993

17 18 19 20

THE LIBRARY OF CONGRESS HAS CATALOGUED THE HARDCOVER
AS FOLLOWS:
Lipton, James.
An exaltation of larks: the ultimate edition/James Lipton.
p. cm.
ISBN 0-670-30044-6 (hc.)
ISBN 0 14 01.7096 0 (pbk.)
1. English language—Terms and phrases. I. Title.
PE1689L5 1991
428.1—dc20   90–50425

Printed in the United States of America
Set in Janson
Designed by Kedakai Lipton

For my mother, Betty Lipton,
who showed me the way to words

Book and Illustration Design

by

Kedakai

Contents

VI

The Game of Venery
Second Move × *287*

I

The Beginning

Most introductory chapters are written in the well-grounded expectation that they will be blithely ignored. Not this one. Let me say hastily that that doesn't argue for its appeal as literature or revelation; but the terrain we will cover has not been widely traveled, and I think a glance through this prefatory Baedeker will significantly heighten the traveler's enjoyment of the journey.

I also hasten to admit that I am not the first explorer in these parts: I see other footprints around me, few and faint, but discernible. Let's begin our journey by following one of those trails. It leads, in a manner of speaking, to Baker Street.

In 1906, thinking he had rid himself once and for all of Holmes and Watson, Sir Arthur Conan Doyle returned to the literary form with which he had begun his career fifteen years earlier, producing a historical novel, *Sir Nigel*. In it the young Nigel comes under the tutelage of Sir John Buttesthorn, the Knight of Duplin, head huntsman to the King, and England's foremost authority on the hunt. In Chapter XI, the sublimely immodest old knight says to Nigel: " 'I take shame that you are not more skilled in the mystery of the woods, seeing that I have had the teaching of you, and that no one in broad England is my master at the craft. I pray you to fill your cup again whilst I make use of the little time that is left to us.' "

There follows a lengthy disquisition on the chase, "with many anecdotes, illustrations, warnings and exceptions, drawn from his own great experience" and finally the knight says, " 'But above all I pray you, Nigel, to have a care in the use of the terms of the craft, lest you should make some blunder at table, so that those who are wiser may have the laugh of you, and we who love you may be shamed.'

" 'Nay, Sir John,' said Nigel. 'I think that after your teaching I can hold my place with the others.'

"The old knight shook his white head doubtfully. 'There is so much to be learned that there is no one who can be said to know it all,' said he. 'For example, Nigel, it is sooth that for every collection of beasts of the forest, and for every gathering of birds of the air, there is their own private name so that none may be confused with another.'

" 'I know it, fair sir.'

" 'You know it, Nigel, but . . . none can say that they know all, though I have myself pricked off eighty and six for a wager at court, and it is said that the chief huntsman of the Duke of Burgundy has counted over a hundred . . . Answer me now, lad, how would you say if you saw ten badgers together in the forest?'

" 'A cete of badgers, fair sir.'

" 'Good, Nigel—good, by my faith! And if you walk in Woolmer Forest and see a swarm of foxes, how would you call it?'

" 'A skulk of foxes.'

" 'And if they lions?'

" 'Nay, fair sir, I am not like to meet several lions in Woolmer Forest.'

" 'Ay, lad, but there are other forests besides Woolmer, and other lands besides England, and who can tell how far afield such a knight errant as Nigel of Tilford may go, when he sees worship to be won? We will say that you were in the deserts of Nubia, and that afterward at the court of the great Sultan you wished to say that you had seen several lions . . . How then would you say it?'

" . . . 'Surely, fair sir, I would be content to say that I had seen a number of lions, if indeed I could say aught after so wondrous an adventure.'

" 'Nay, Nigel, a huntsman would have said that he had seen a pride of lions, and so proved that he knew the language of the chase. Now, had it been boars instead of lions?'

" 'One says a singular of boars.'

" 'And if they be swine?'

" 'Surely it is a herd of swine.'

" 'Nay, nay, lad, it is indeed sad to see how little you know . . . No man of gentle birth would speak of a herd of swine; that is the peasant speech. If you drive them it is a herd. If you hunt them it is other. What call you them then, Edith?'

" 'Nay, I know not.'

" . . . 'But you can tell us, Mary?'

" 'Surely, sweet sir, one talks of a sounder of swine.'

"The old Knight laughed exultantly. 'Here is a pupil who never brings me shame! . . . Hark ye! only last week that jack-fool, the young Lord of Brocas, was here talking of having seen a covey of pheasants in the wood. One such speech would have been the ruin of a young squire at the court. How would you have said it, Nigel?'

" 'Surely, fair sir, it should be a nye of pheasants.'

" 'Good Nigel—a nye of pheasants, even as it is a gaggle of geese or a badling of ducks, a fall of woodcock or a wisp of snipe. But a covey of pheasants! What sort of talk is that?' "

What sort indeed! This quotation from Conan Doyle makes, for me, the central point about the first four parts of this book: the terms you will find here are authentic; that is, each of them, as fanciful—and even frivolous—as some of them may seem, was at one time either in general use as the *only* proper term for a group of whatever beast, fish, fowl or insect it designated,[1] or had acquired sufficient currency to warrant its inclusion in a list with the well-established hunting terms.

1: Then, as now, as the quotation from Conan Doyle indicates, one would show truly ludicrous ignorance by referring to a herd of fish or a school of elephants.

Obviously, at one time or another, every one of these terms had to be invented—and it is also obvious that much imagination, wit and semantic ingenuity has always gone into that invention: the terms are so charming and poetic it is hard to believe their inventors were unaware of the possibilities open to them, and unconscious of the fun and beauty they were creating. What we have in these terms is clearly the end result of a game that amateur philologists have been playing for over five hundred years.

Bear in mind that most of these terms were codified in the fifteenth century,[1] a time when the English language was in the process of an expansion—or more accurately, explosion—that can only be compared in importance and scope to the intellectual effusions of Periclean Greece or cinquecento Italy.

The Encyclopædia Britannica describes as "peculiar to English . . . the extreme receptiveness of its vocabulary to borrowings from other languages." The inhabitants of the island we now call Britain have always shown an astonishing verbal amenability, a quite childlike open-mindedness to and delight in the new. Elizabeth Drew, former Chairman of the Department of English at Smith College, has written about the English language, ". . . no other can communicate such subtle shades of thought and feeling, such fine discriminations of meaning. The riches of its mingled derivations supply a multitude of synonyms . . . so that *fatherly* is not the same as *paternal*, nor *fortune* as *luck*, nor *boyish* as *puerile* . . ."

I admit to a prejudice toward my own language (and a regrettable inability to read Tolstoi, Dante and the T'ang poets in their original tongues), but I think a good case can be made for English as the preeminent literary language. Compare it to any other; for example, French. Set the starting point of our literary race at the year 1500, the finish-line at 1700. Who shall represent France?—Rabelais, Ronsard, Du Bellay, Jodelle, Montaigne, Malherbe, Corneille, Pascal, Molière, La Rochefoucauld, Boileau, Racine, La Fontaine, Bossuet, Madame de Sévigné and La Bruyère. This list of two hundred years of French literary genius is generous and comprehensive. Now, let us handicap English by giving French a hundred years' head start; we will set the English starting line at *1600*. In the hundred years that followed it, the English literary genius produced Campion, Donne, Dekker, Beaumont, Lovelace, Jonson, Herrick, Webster, Herbert, Shakespeare, Suckling, Crashaw, Milton, Marvell, Dryden, Bacon, Raleigh, Bunyan, Walton, Pepys, and the forty-seven inspired translators of the King James Bible.[2]

1: *The Egerton Manuscript*, the earliest surviving list of them, dates from about 1450; *The Book of St. Albans*, the most complete and important of the early lists (and the seminal source for most subsequent compilations), appeared in 1486.

2: Excluded from the list as a further handicap are such giants as Pope, Defoe and Swift whose *major* works appeared after 1700.

I am well aware that this kind of contest is in a sense invidious; how do you compare one writer's genius with another's, Molière's, for example, with Shakespeare's, or Dante's with Cervantes'? The answer, of course, is that you don't and shouldn't. But the oeuvre of two different periods, or two nations, *can* be compared, and on this basis I think that the literary production of any nation, ranged alongside English, may find itself shadowed. And, finally, I think that the richness of English as a literary language can best be explained by the unique flexibility and omnivorous word-hunger of the generations of Britons who forged the uncommonly keen sword wielded by our belletristic heroes.

An accident of geography played a large part in the process. The British Isle, lying fat and fecund behind a low, beckoning coastline and narrow, unforbidding moat, was an irresistible lure to the peoples of the mainland. G. M. Trevelyan, in his *History of England*, a book as admirable for its literary style as for its historiology, says, "The temptation to invade the island lay not in the pearls, the gold and the tin for which it seems to have been noted . . . long before the foundation of Rome; temptation lay also in its fertile soil, the rich carpet of perennial green that covered the downs and every clearing in the forest, the absence of long interludes of frost that must have seemed miraculous in a land so far to the North before men knew the secret of the Gulf Stream."

And with each new wave of traders or invaders came new semantic blood, new ideas and new ways of expressing them. The narrow, languid brook of the Celtic tongue suddenly acquired a powerful tributary as the splendid geometry of the Latin language burst into it, bringing such lofty sounds and concepts as *intellect, fortune, philosophy, education, victory, gratitude.* From 449 on, the blunt, intensely expressive monosyllables of the Anglo-Saxons joined the swelling stream, giving us the names of the strong, central elements of our lives: *God, earth, sun, sea, win, lose, live, love* and *die.* Then, in the eleventh century, with the Norman Conquest, a great warm gush of French sonorities—*emotion, pity, peace, devotion, romance*—swelled the torrent to a flood-tide that burst its banks, spreading out in broad, loamy deltas black with the rich silt of **WORDS**.

It was in precisely this word-hungry, language-mad England that the terms you will encounter in this book were born. They are prime examples of both the infinite subtlety of our language and the wild imagination and verbal skill of our forebears. The terms were codified during the period when the river of words was approaching its greatest breadth, beginning in about 1450 with *The Egerton Manuscript*.

These terms and phrases, like the other verbal inventions of their time, were not idly made, but were intended for, and in many cases achieved, wide currency and acceptance. As you will see in Part II of this book, a number of them have come down to this day, and are accepted, taken-for-granted figures of speech. What is most remarkable to me about this rich repository of poetry is that all the terms in it can be said to be correct, proper, and usable. The lyrical, fanciful EXALTATION OF LARKS has credentials as good as the mundane and universally accepted SCHOOL OF FISH, since both terms offer as provenance the same source, the list in *The Book of St. Albans.* The fact is that AN EXALTATION OF LARKS is the 18th term in the list and A SCHOOL OF FISH is the 132nd. Such whimsies as A SHREWDNESS OF APES and A COWARDICE OF CURS also precede the more familiar fish term (109th and 117th).[1]

So, one can certainly argue with good logic that *every* one of the terms you will find in Parts II and III of this book has an equal claim on our respect and loyalty. The fact that many of them have slipped out of our common speech can only, I think, be described as lamentable. There is little enough poetry in our speech (and lives) to continue to ignore a vein as rich as this. The purpose of this book is to try, in an admittedly modest measure, to redress the balance. The thesis of this book can be summed up very simply: when a group of ravens flaps by, you should, if you want to refer to their presence, say, "There goes an unkindness of ravens." Anything else would be wrong.

The reader may have noticed that, until this moment, I have avoided giving a single, comprehensive collective term to these collective terms. That is because there isn't any. Oddly enough, the compilers of the numerous lists of these words, though obviously enthusiastic philologists, have never felt compelled to settle on a term for them. The explorer in this field will find these words referred to as "nouns of multitude," "company terms," "nouns of assemblage," "collective nouns,"[2] "group terms," and "terms of venery." This last seems to me best and most appropriate, and itself warrants some explanation.

"Venery" and its adjective, "venereal," are most often thought of, of course, as signifying love, specifically physical love. From *Venus* we have the Latin root *ven* which appears in the word *venari*, meaning "to hunt game." Eric Partridge, in his etymological dictionary *Origins*, asserts that the *ven* in *venari* has its original meaning: "to desire (and therefore) to pursue," and he sees a close connection between it and the word "win," from the Middle English *winnen*, and even the Sanskrit *vanoti*, "he conquers." It is in this sense that venery came to signify the hunt, and it was so used in all the early works on the chase, including the earliest known on the subject of

---

1: There are a number of expressions in our contemporary speech that have the form of these terms and obviously derive from the order. We will encounter them shortly.

2: I hold this to be a misnomer since, obviously, it can be confused with the strictly grammatical term referring to such words as "majority." The same may be said of "nouns of multitude."

English hunting, *Le Art de Venery*, written in Norman French in the 1320's by Edward II's huntsman, Master William Twici.

So, if all the earlier, more knowledgeable experts in this field have left it to someone of the twentieth century to select the proper term for these proper terms, I (cautiously and with boundless and well-founded humility) pick up the gauntlet and declare for "terms of venery," if for no more cogent reason than that it smacks more of the field than the classroom, and, in its adjectival form, more of Gomorrah than Grammar.

So be it. Henceforward we are talking about terms of venery or—occasionally, judiciously, disingenuously—venereal terms.

Before beginning the list of authentic terms, a word is in order on the etymological differences among them. The venereal Order seems to me to break down into six Families, according to the apparent inspiration for each term. I would list the six Families as:

1: *Onomatopoeia:* for example, A MURMURATION OF STARLINGS, A GAGGLE OF GEESE.

2: *Characteristic:* A LEAP OF LEOPARDS, A SKULK OF FOXES. By far the largest family.

3: *Appearance:* A KNOT OF TOADS, A PARLIAMENT OF OWLS.

4: *Habitat:* A SHOAL OF BASS, A NEST OF RABBITS.

5: *Comment* (pro or con, reflecting the observer's point of view): A RICHNESS OF MARTENS, A COWARDICE OF CURS.

6: *Error* (resulting from an incorrect transcription by a scribe or printer, faithfully preserved in the corrupted form by subsequent compilers): A SCHOOL OF FISH, originally "shoal."

The preceding six Families of venereal terms are my construction. In the lists that follow I will not indicate to which Family I would assign each term, preferring to leave it to the reader to decide whether A MURDER OF CROWS belongs in the second or fifth Family. These decisions are proper moves in the game of venery.

All of the authentic terms you are about to encounter received their first official stamp in the so-called Books of Courtesy, medieval and fifteenth-century social primers, intended, as the quotation from *Sir Nigel* indicates, to provide a gentleman with the means of social acceptability, and to spare him the embarrassment of "some blunder at table, so that those who are wiser may have the laugh of you, and we who love you may be shamed."[1] The Books dealt with a variety of subjects, but in the largely rural England

---

1: William Blades, in his Introduction to the 1881 facsimile edition of *The Book of St. Albans*, refers to the book's subjects as "those with which, at that period, every man claiming to be 'gentle' was expected to be familiar; while ignorance of their laws and language was to confess himself a 'churl.' "

of that time, the section on the Hunt was doubtless the most important. And in nearly all the Books of Courtesy, the authors saw fit to transcribe a list of the proper, accepted terms of venery. After *Egerton* (the earliest surviving manuscript, referred to earlier), most of the lists were based on previous compilations, always with some omissions, errors and additions. In spite of this variance, each succeeding list gave greater weight of authority to the terms. In the fifteenth century there were several important manuscripts containing lists of terms. In addition to the *Egerton*, which contained one hundred six terms, there were two *Harley Manuscripts*, with forty-eight terms in the first and forty-five in the second, *The Porkington Manuscript*, with one hundred nine, *The Digby* and *The Robert of Gloucester Manuscripts*, each with fifty.

The subject was of such importance that, in about 1476, within a year of the establishment of printing in England, a printed book, *The Hors, Shepe, & The Ghoos*, appeared, with a list of one hundred six venereal terms. But by far the most important of the early works on the subject was *The Book of St. Albans*, with its one hundred sixty-four terms, printed in 1486 at St. Albans by "the schoolmaster printer."

The accredited author was, interestingly, a woman, Dame Juliana Barnes, reputedly the sister of Lord Berners and prioress of the nunnery of Sopewell. There has, however, been considerable debate on the identity of Dame Juliana, with some authorities insisting she was a pure invention and others arguing strenuously for her existence. William Blades, the expert on early English printing cited on the preceding page, came out staunchly for Dame Juliana in his Introduction to the facsimile edition of *The Book of St. Albans*. In it he inveighs against most of her biographers for only adding to the mystery with their highly imaginative accounts of her life. At one point a "scholar" read her name as Julyan and produced a learned biography of a man. So she remained, writes Blades, until "Chauncy, in 1700 (History of Hertfordshire) restored her sex . . . and then set to work upon making a family for her. His first discovery was that, being a 'Dame,' she was of noble blood. Finding also that the family name of Lord Berners was, in olden time, spelt occasionally Barnes, he soon supplied a father for our authoress, in the person of Sir James Berners. And so the game of making history went on merrily. . . . But enough of such sham biography; let us return to facts. The word 'Dame' did not in the fifteenth century . . . imply any connection with a titled family, it meant simply Mistress or Mrs. . . . Allowing that Lord Berners' name was sometimes spelt Barnes, is that sufficient reason for making our authoress a member of his family? I think not."

Having disposed of falsehood, Blades argues for the truth of Dame Juliana's existence, largely from internal evidence in the Book, finally committing himself to the extent of pronouncing her "England's earliest poetess."

He allows for the possibility that two parts of the Book, on Hawking and Heraldry, may be the work of the anonymous "schoolmaster printer," but he grants Dame Juliana undisputed authorship of the part on Hunting (the one with which we are concerned).

Other authorities have held that the entire *Book of St. Albans* is nothing but a compilation of earlier works and folk material, put together by one or several printers under the collective *nom de guerre* of Dame Juliana. At this distance we cannot decide the matter, and so it seems that Dame Juliana is doomed to suffer the literary fate of Homer (there could be worse). Whether Homer was one blind poet or several generations of nameless bards, and whether Dame Juliana was a lone and quite extraordinary prioress or A PLAGIARY OF PRINTERS in the fifteenth century, the important fact remains that *The Book of St. Albans* is the definitive work on the subject at hand, and fascinating by any standard.[1]

It contains three parts, the first on Hawking, the second on Hunting, and the third on Heraldry. The book on Hawking contains such paragraph headings as "A medecyne for an hawke that has loſt here courage."[2] and "The maner how a man ſhall put an hawke in to mewe—and that is to be wele nooted."

The first book ends by assigning certain hawks to certain ranks, thus: "Theys hawkes belong to an Emproure . . . Theis hawkes belong to a kyng . . . For a prince . . . For a duke . . . For an erle . . . for a Baron . . . Hawkes for a knyght . . . Hawkis for a Squyer[3] . . . For a lady[4] . . . An hawke for a young man," and the section concludes with "And yit ther be moo kyndis of hawkes," listing them, then closes with "*Explicit.*"[5]

The second book, the one that concerns us, on Hunting, begins with a brief foreword by Dame Juliana: "Lyke Wiſe as i the booke of hawkying aforeſayd . . ." "Likewise, as in the book of hawking aforesaid are written and noted the terms of pleasure belonging to gentlemen having delight therein, in the same manner this book following showeth to such gentle persons the manner of hunting for all manner of beasts, whether they be

---

1: In 1496, the famous and aptly named Wynken de Worde (the aptness is no coincidence: his real name was Jan van Wynken), successor to the first English printer, William Caxton, reprinted *The Book of St. Albans*, and in the sixteenth century there were more than a dozen new editions of the book.

2: In this section I have occasionally retained the language of the Book, with its long s's and its "ys" and "is" plurals, to impart the flavor of the original. Since the contemporary eye adjusts slowly to the dusk of fifteenth century orthography, the murkier passages will be modernized.

3: These variant spellings, Theys and Theis, Hawkes and Hawkis, sometimes occurring in the same line of text, are common in early English printing.

4: Each of these headings is followed by a list of the proper hawks, *e.g.*, "Ther is a Merlyon. And that hawke is for a lady."

5: An abbreviation of *explicitus est liber*, "the book is unfolded" (from the time when it was in fact a rolled parchment). It usually appears in colophons with the author's name, and is simply a fifteenth-century way of signifying The End.

beasts of venery, or of chase, or Rascal.[1] And also it showeth all the terms convenient as well to the hounds as to the beasts aforesaid. And in certain there be many diverse of them as it is declared in the book following."

There follow two septets, a form popularized a hundred years earlier by Chaucer, each comprising three rhymed couplets and an internally rhymed concluding line. The first septet is called "Beſtýs of venerý," the second "Beſtýs of the Chace."

The entire book is addressed to "My dere chylde" (in the second line of the opening poem). Further in the text we encounter such phrases as "Do so, my child," "Think what I say, my son," etc. This maternal tone is one of the most frequently advanced arguments for Dame Juliana's authorship.

The book continues almost entirely in verse, with such titles as "What is a bevý of Roos grete or ſmall" and "The rewarde for howndýs." It contains a very long poem called "How ýe ſhall breeche an hert," with explicit instructions for removing "the finale gutties . . . the leuer [liver] . . . and after that the bledder . . ." and concludes on the recto of sig. tiiij (the 24th page) with "Explicit Dam Julyans Barnes in her boke of huntyng." Though this would seem to end the book, in fact, and luckily, it does not. Because of Dame Juliana's colophon here there has been some argument as to the authorship of the seven pages following it which conclude the book of Hunting and contain, among other things, the famous venereal list. This is one of the principal reasons that the schoolmaster printer sometimes shares creative credit with the prioress.

Whatever their authorship, the seven pages contain treatises in both poetry and prose on such subjects as "The propreteis of a goode Grehound" and "The propretees [*sic*, another example of variant spelling] of a goode hors," followed by a battery of maxims and homilies under the heading "Merke wele theýs iiii thýnges." One of the things to be marked well is:

Too Wyues in oon hous [Two women in one house], too cattys and oon mous. Too dogges and oon boon: Theis ſhall neu accord I oon.

And then, on the facing recto page, we find the title "The Compaýnýs of beſtýs and fowlýs," followed by two vertical columns beginning with "An Herde of Hertis" (harts), and continuing, in fifteenth-century English,

---

1: The four beasts of venery were the red deer (hart and hind), hare, boar and wolf. The four beasts of the chase were the fallow deer (buck and doe), fox, marten and roe. C. E. Hare, in *The Language of Field Sports*, writes that "rascal" originally meant "rabble" or "mob," and that it was a hunting term "applied to all beasts other than the four beasts of venery, and the four beasts of the chase." All three groups were locked into a rigid hierarchic order. Conan Doyle's Knight of Duplin is firm on the subject: "He also spoke of the several ranks and grades of the chase: how the hare, hart, and boar must ever take precedence over the buck, the doe, the fox, the marten and the roe, even as a knight banneret does over a knight, while these in turn are of a higher class to the badger, the wildcat, or the otter, who are but the common populace of the world of beasts."

through an exhaustive list of one hundred sixty-four venereal terms, some surprising, some amusing, and some arrestingly beautiful. The most surprising thing about the list is that not all of the terms in it refer to beeſtys and fowlys. Of Dame Juliana's (or the schoolmaster printer's) astonishing digressions into the realm of poetry and wit, more will be said in Part IV. For the moment, we will confine ourselves to the authentic terms of the hunt, compiled from the seminal *Book of St. Albans* and its fellow manuscripts and books on the subject.

When the first edition of *An Exaltation of Larks* appeared, I went to some pains to point out that the lists of venery in the book weren't intended as etymology or zoology. "None of these musings," I wrote, "pretend to a high order of scholarship. They are at most an innocent ramble through unfamiliar fields." Time has proven me wrong about the latter assertion: the innocent ramble became a journey, then a quest, and finally a crusade, the record of which the reader will find in Part III—and on every subsequent page of the book.

While I underestimated *An Exaltation of Larks'* etymological intent and impact, I have always felt that, if the book is anything more than the caprice that meets the eye, it is modestly literary, in the sense that T. S. Eliot once described literature as "the impulse to transcribe one's thoughts correctly." The heart and soul of this book is the concern that our language, one of our most precious natural resources, is also a dwindling one that deserves at least as much protection as our woodlands, wetlands and whooping cranes.

With the keenest, most powerful linguistic instrument on the planet at our disposal, our language shrinks, not at the highest level of intellectual life, where the endangered species is bred and kept alive, like Siberian tigers in a zoo, but at nearly every level below it. Motion pictures, radio and television, contemporary language's primary delivery systems, deliberately, by tacit fiat, make do with the vocabulary of the common denominator toward which they are aimed, a legitimate business strategy, a damaging linguistic one. By the age of nineteen, the average American has logged 11,000 hours in school and 15,000 hours in front of the television tube, listening to the same few hundred hackneyed words in listless rotation. When the latest National Assessment of Educational Progress was released, the Education Secretary declared the reading and writing skills of American students "dreadfully inadequate."

This is not to place the blame on television or motion pictures. They are the emblematic art-forms of our time, and when they are good they are unmatchable. But they are, and should be, *pictures*. "You writers," complains Larry Gelbart's movie producer in the musical comedy *City of Angels*, "words, words, words!" In Shakespeare's *Henry VI, Part II*, the rebel Jack Cade upbraids the Lord Say with "Thou hast most traitorously corrupted the youth of the realm in erecting a grammar-school; and whereas, before, our forefathers had no other books but the score and the tally, thou hast caused printing to be used; and contrary to the king, his crown and dignity, thou hast built a paper-mill. It will be proved to thy face that thou hast men about thee that usually talk of a noun and a verb, and such abominable words as no Christian ear can endure to hear." With this, Cade sends the luckless Treasurer to the headsman.

If Shakespeare, whose authorship of all of the three-part Henry VI has been questioned, put those words in Jack Cade's mouth, he was grinding an axe sharper than the headsman's, which he wielded as few authors have before or since. His answer to the Neanderthals' logophobia was: more nouns and verbs. If he "wrote down" to the groundlings, it was only spatially.

What shall *our* answer be, in a world in which two generations have grown up facing screens, large and small, to the point where the picture is not only *worth* a thousand words, it has ended by virtually replacing them, leading management expert Peter Drucker to conclude, "the printed book is primarily a tool for adults. The new tools . . . are for children." Wordless, it seems, we will build the new Jerusalem.

I propose instead a language sanctuary, a wild-word refuge, removed and safe from the hostile environment of our TV-tabloid world. And as long as we are still enmeshed in the encumbering toils of language, I am hopeful that this book with its more than 1,100 terms of venery, will, to however modest a degree, expand our means of performing the difficult, important feat of transferring a thought from one mind to another. I assume this is an important task, else why would Eliot be concerned about transcribing his "thoughts correctly," or W. H. Auden have quoted the child who asked, "How can I know what I think 'til I see what I say?" or Dylan Thomas have written, "I hack/This rumpus of shapes[1]/For you to know/How I, a spinning man,/Glory also this star . . ."? Wordsworth, in the famous *Preface to the Second Edition of Lyrical Ballads* in which he formulated the often quoted definition of poetry as "emotion recollected in tranquility," even had the audacity to describe the poet as "a man speaking to men." Coleridge muttered stubbornly that poetry was "the best words in their best order," and even the angels are on our side (or vice versa), for we find "How forcible are right words" in Job 6:25, and "A word fitly spoken is like apples of gold in pictures of silver" in Proverbs 25:11. Hart Crane, in an excess of logophilic zeal that would have earned him the contempt of some of our contemporary theorists, dared to exclaim, "One must be drenched in words, literally soaked in them,

---

1: Note, in passing, the venereal term. They are not uncommon in Dylan's work. See Cases In Point.

to have the right ones form themselves into the proper patterns at the right moment," and in the *Four Quartets* Eliot admits that "Our concern was speech, and speech impelled us/To purify the language of the tribe." High contemporary marks to Mr. Eliot for the tribal reference, but F for putting so high a value on the soon-to-be debased coinage of language.[1]

There *are* areas, such as science and slang, in which our language continues to grow, as stubbornly as weeds in cracked cement. Certainly the language of the laboratory and launching pad has invaded our common speech, and some of the words and phrases we use freely have a transcendental beauty: *supersonic, module, cyclotron, isotope, helix, meson, photon* . . . even *ballistic missile*, which, in spite of its ominous significance, has a stunning echoic sound. To mathemeticians, an ingenious solution is "elegant;" and in 1961, physicist Murray Gell-Mann borrowed James Joyce's mysterious "Three quarks for Muster Mark" to name the equally mysterious particles that were popping up in accelerators. Matters continued to improve as physicists decided that quarks come in six "flavors," up, down, strange, charmed, bottom and top, and that each flavor comes in three "colors"—a far cry from the ponderous scientific sobriety that used to insist on Greek and Latin montrosities with all the lightfooted charm of *eccentroösteochondrodysplasia*.

In the 1960s and 70's it looked as though the mother tongue might be significantly enriched by slang, especially the sinuous patois of the African American and his mimics in the jazz and rock worlds and among the young, the hip and the would-be hip. The collapse of England's social barriers in the democratizing wake of the Second World War opened the sluices to a millrace of lively provincial dialects, attitudes and words. Oxonians affected Liverpudlian. In both England and the United States, popular music, this century's great folk art, introduced daring new themes and ways of expressing them, and for a time it seemed that the most innovative writers and performers had abandoned Tin Pan Alley's aging orthodoxies for Rimbaud's visionary illuminations. But with the entrepeneurial lords of music—and motion pictures—reaching for, and catering to, a younger and younger audience, the revolution that began so promisingly aged paradoxically and prematurely, its refreshing shower of coinage congealing to clichés as shopworn as the words they had elbowed aside.

The young can't be blamed for going with the flow: pollution flows downstream, and when *Time Magazine* mutters that the President's "assaults against English included telling fellow economic summiteers that 'a new world of freedom lays before us,' " it is evident that verbal imprecision begins at a society's headwaters. On the page and the airwaves carelessness

---

1: A genuine F, perhaps, for "borrowing" *Donner un sens plus pur aux mots de la tribu*, without acknowledging its author, Mallarmé.

is erasing the boundaries between *in lieu of* and *in light of*; *feel different* and *feel differently*; *more important* and *more importantly*. *Hopefully* is marching roughshod through sentences, modifying every word on the Eleven O'Clock News but the right one. Forty years ago Oscar Hammerstein grumbled that, if *as* and *like* were interchangeable, Shakespeare would have called it *Like You Like It*; it's as well Hammerstein didn't live to hear today's ubiquitous "like." *Quite unique, less perfect* and *most fatal* are reduced to absurdity by adding qualifiers to unmodifiable adjectives. We are in danger of forgetting that *presently* is "soon," *at present* is "now;" *appraise* isn't *apprise; averse* isn't *adverse; imply* isn't *infer; comprise* can't live with "of" and *composed* can't live without it; *bemused* is "confused," not *amused; penultimate* isn't beyond *ultimate*, it's just short of it; *kind* is singular, so, "*that* kind of boys" is on the mark, and the fashionable "*these kinds* of boys," making both words safely plural, is a cowardly dodge; as is the equally pusillanimous *myself*, to avoid the daunting choice of *me* or *I* after a preposition; and *careen* isn't *career*. Trust Stephen Sondheim to get it brilliantly right: in *Follies*, the faded star Carlotta notes that you "career from career to career."

Do these dour linguistic cavils matter? The critic and gadfly Alexander Woollcott thought so. When a soprano replied to his criticism of her performance with, "I'd like to hear *him* sing that aria," Woollcott sighed, "In moments of stress, people are so imprecise." In the summer of 1990, *Time Magazine* announced in a bright yellow box that "this week we'll be making some changes. In the past we have spelled out the numbers zero through twelve; now we'll use figures for 10, 11 and 12. We used to capitalize the word *Government* . . . now we will capitalize it only when it appears with the word Federal. *Kidnapping* will be spelled with two *p*s. These modifications are not as trivial as they seem. They reflect our constant monitoring of a living language . . ." And John Hodgkin ends his monumental *Proper Terms*, which you will soon meet, with an unexplained, unattributed, unapologetic, "Lerne or be Lewde."

Words, said T. S. Eliot, "slip, slide, perish/Decay with imprecision, will not stay in place,/Will not stay still," and Elizabeth Drew (whom I have quoted earlier) has written, "Language is like soil. However rich, it is subject to erosion, and its fertility is constantly threatened by uses that exhaust its vitality. It needs constant re-invigoration if it is not to become arid and sterile. Poetry is one great source of the maintenance and renewal of language."

And the poetry need not come exclusively from poets. In fact, the poet and critic Louis Untermeyer has written, "We cannot escape from poetry. We needs its power of quick communication in every casual activity . . . The very man who belittles poetry in public practices it in private . . . His dreams are poetry . . . his simplest sentences rely on the power of imagery . . . we delight to intensify a hard drizzle by saying 'it's raining cats and dogs.' . . . [A] good servant is not merely rare but 'scarce as hen's teeth,' . . . The fruit-grower . . . capitalizes the power of poetry by saying that [his oranges] are *Sunkist*, a conceit worthy of the Elizabethan singers . . . The architect daringly suggests the tower of Babel with the 'skyscraper'; the man in the street intensifies his speech by tightening it into slang, the shorthand of the people, by 'crashing' a party, 'muscling' in, 'hitting' the high spots. Language is continually being made swift and powerful through the medium of the poetic phrase."

So, here are some new candidates for our contemporary lexicon— the trophies of the long, exciting search that began when I realized with an exhilharating shiver that GAGGLE OF GEESE and PRIDE OF LIONS might not be just isolated pools of amusing poetic idiosyncrasy but estuaries leading to a virtually uncharted sea, sparkling with found poetry—and intriguing poetic possibilities. Every curious soul has its moment on that peak in Darien. That was mine and it led to these pages.

I have two earnest hopes: one, that the evangelistic tone of this preface will be forgiven; and, two, that a few of the terms from Parts III and IV— and even from Part V—will stick to our ribs and be ingested into our speech. If they do, it isn't just that we will be able to turn to someone and coolly and correctly say, "Look—a charm of finches." What is more important is that a charm of poetry will have slipped quietly into our lives.

II

The Known

This list contains some of the terms of venery that are a part of our living speech. Many of them are as old as the terms in Parts III and IV, but since we still use them, I have separated them from their brothers and sisters.

They may be so familiar that we say or read them without thinking: they have lost their poetry for us. But step back for a moment from some of these familiar terms—A PLAGUE OF LOCUSTS, A PRIDE OF LIONS, A LITTER OF PUPS (plague! pride! *litter!*)—and perhaps their aptness and daring will reappear.

So with all the terms in this part: we begin on familiar ground, to sharpen our senses by restoring the magic to the mundane.

A SCHOOL OF FISH

As *noted earlier,* school *was a corruption of* shoal, *a term still in use for specific fish (see Part III). C. E. Hare, in* The Language of Field Sports, *quotes John Hodgkin on this term arguing that* school *and* shoal *are in fact variant spellings of the same word, but Eric Partridge, I think correctly, sees them coming from two different roots, the former from ME* scole, *deriving from the Latin* schola, *a school, and the latter from the OE* sceald, *meaning shallow. I think it is obvious that in the lexicon of venery* shoal *was meant and* school *is a corruption.*

A CATCH OF FISH
Deceased.

A PACK OF DOGS

A LITTER OF PUPS

A MONTH OF SUNDAYS

A MOUNTAIN OF DEBT

A HILL OF BEANS

A DOSE OF SALTS

A PRIDE OF LIONS

One of the oldest venereal terms, antedating even the English lists in the French lyons orgeuilleux. *The earliest English manuscript,* Egerton, *and* The Book of St. Albans *both have a* Pryde of Lyons.

A HERD OF ELEPHANTS

A NEST OF VIPERS
Also, generation of vipers, *Jesus's characterization of the multitude that came to be baptized. "O* generation of vipers, *who hath warned you to flee from the wrath to come?"* Luke, 3:7.

A BARREL OF MONKEYS

A FIELD OF RACEHORSES

A HERD OF HORSES
A STRING OF PONIES
A BROOD OF HENS
A RUN OF POULTRY
A FLOCK OF SHEEP
A TEAM OF OXEN
Dating from the fifteenth century Harley Manuscript.

A CLOUD OF GRASSHOPPERS

Or GNATS

A SWARM OF BEES

A NEST OF WASPS

A PLAGUE OF LOCUSTS

A COLONY OF ANTS

AN ARMY OF CATERPILLARS

A BUNCH OF GRAPES

A HAND OF BANANAS

A SHEAF OF WHEAT
Sheaves are stalks of grain tied together.

A SHOCK OF CORN
A shock is a pile of sheaves of grain or stalks of corn propped in a field. See thrave of threshers.

A BENCH OF JUDGES

A COLLEGE OF CARDINALS

A BOARD OF TRUSTEES

A FIELD OF RUNNERS

A GANG OF LABORERS

A LINE OF SOVEREIGNS

AN ORDER OF PEERS

A COVEN OF WITCHES (FEMALE)

A CONGERIES OF WITCHES (MALE)

A GATHERING OF CLANS

A POSSE OF VIGILANTES

From the Latin posse comitatus, *power of the county, those citizens subject to callup by an English sheriff in times of trouble. In America's Old West the term—and custom—were given considerable latitude.*

A BEVY OF BEAUTIES

This is one of the few terms of venery whose origin is uncertain. Hodgkin says, "There is no satisfactory etymology for the word 'bevy.'" Partridge marks it o.o.o.—of obscure origin; but hazards the guess that it derives from the Old French bevée, *a drink or drinking.*

A BAND OF MEN
Hence also band *for a group of musicians.*

A SLATE OF CANDIDATES
Doubtless deriving from the time when nominees' names were chalked on one.

A CONSTITUENCY OF VOTERS

A COLLEGE OF ELECTORS

A CONGREGATION OF PEOPLE

A PASSEL OF BRATS
An American term, of course. J. Donald Adams went looking for this one, finding it finally in Wentworth's American Dialect Dictionary *as "hull passel of young ones," "a passel o' hogs," etc., but no etymology is given. A Southern friend assures me, however, that* passel *is simply "parcel" in a regional dialect.*

A HOST OF ANGELS

An interesting term this. J. Donald Adams, in The Magic and Mystery of Words, *says, "Angels in any quantity may be referred to only as a* host. *The word's title to that distinction is clear enough;* host *derives from the Latin* hostis, *meaning enemy, and hence came to mean an army. It was presumably applied to angels as the warriors of God."*

A HAIL OF GUNFIRE

A FUSILLADE OF BULLETS

A NEST OF MACHINE GUNS

A BARRAGE OF SHELLS

A BAPTISM OF FIRE

A QUIVER OF ARROWS

At the beginning of this section, I suggested we step back from these familiar terms, to experience them anew. This candidate for reevaluation can be found as a quiver of arrows *in Psalters dated as early as 1300; which tells us that more than seven hundred years ago someone, who could have used the familiar thirteenth-century words* case *or* scabbard, *arbitrarily and whimsically turned* quiver *into a noun—and a timeless portrait of an arrow trembling in its target.*

A CHORUS OF COMPLAINT

A TISSUE OF LIES
Also, pack.

A DEN OF THIEVES

A CAN OF WORMS

A HEAD OF STEAM

A FLEET OF SHIPS

A SET OF CHINA

Since, as noted on the preceding page, the purpose of this section is to restore the magic to the mundane by reexamining words we take for granted, let's see what happens when we put our magnifying glass over the commonest *of these common* terms, set. *Any surprises? Yes: the* Oxford English Dictionary *devotes 23 pages* (sic) *to the word! "The complete collection of the 'pieces' composing a suite of furniture, a service of china, a clothing outfit, or the like," descended from the Old French* sette, *is there, as is a set of badgers* (q.v.)—*but so are hundreds of other definitions, nuances, roots and tributaries. The point of this note is that the intrepid semanticist in search of any word's meaning may find himself hacking his way through an Amazonian jungle of possibilities. And that, as every page of this book attests, is the great and everlasting glory of the vast, supple, subtle English language.*

A PEAL OF BELLS

A FLIGHT OF STAIRS

A PATTER OF FOOTSTEPS

A ROUND OF DRINKS

A ROPE OF PEARLS

A BOUQUET OF FLOWERS

AN EMBARRASSMENT OF RICHES

A CONSTELLATION OF STARS

A PENCIL OF LINES
A proper contemporary group term in mathematics.

A BILL OF PARTICULARS

A MESS OF POTTAGE

III

The Unknown

The quest that led to this book began, fittingly, in the Reading Room of the British Museum, where, clutching my Temporary Reader's Ticket and surrounded by the ghosts of the great literary, philosophical and political personages who had haunted that sacred precinct in life, I signed a request for what was, to my knowledge, the only extant copy of *The Book of St. Albans*.

I was ushered to the kind of small, sealed inner chamber in which Tiffany shows its best jewels to its best customers—or San Quentin gasses its worst malefactors. A uniformed guard arrived with the book, and remained at the door as I opened the book to pages I had seen only on microfilm . . . and so the adventure began.

When *An Exaltation of Larks* was published in 1968, in a modest edition of 5,000 copies, it contained 118 pages and approximately 175 terms, authentic and fanciful, the former wrestled, as Mark Twain characterized his translation back from French of *The Celebrated Jumping Frog of Calaveras County*, from Middle to Modern English. Working with all the resources then at my command, I grappled with the mysteries of the *blecche of sowters* and *kerff of panteris* I found in the fifteenth century books and manuscripts. Some yielded to my research, some did not. The contemporary terms came with relative ease: a SLOUCH OF MODELS sprang on the scene, followed by a LURCH OF BUSES and a WINCE OF DENTISTS. Inventing them was like eating peanuts: I found it hard to stop. And to everyone's astonishment, not least mine, so did the public. In 1968, I thought of my hoard of terms of venery as a linguistic rear guard, digging in for a last-ditch stand against the massed battalions of the anti-verbal army looming smug and strong in every direction—led by the perdurable Jack Cade. But I am delighted to report that the faint sound of a fusty bugle accompanied the appearance on the horizon of an antic troop, trailing caissons of words. Emerging from the cracks, crannies, fissures, caves and assorted secret places to which an antilexic world had driven them, they charged to the rescue, bearing everything from a single treasured invention to a tapeworm of terms. Textbooks challenged students to join the game of venery, and the students' responses brought fresh bursts of inspiration to my doorstep. Contributors to every sort of periodical used the book like sourdough, to leaven new batchs of terms; newspaper and magazine columnists, and radio and television programs entered the lists, literally and figuratively. Posters, T-shirts and a set of engraved crystal glasses appeared.

The first printing mushroomed to a second, a fifth, a tenth, a twelfth. The book was accorded a signal honor: in twenty-three years it has never gone out of print, in hardcover or paperback . . . and now it is back, in this Ultimate Edition of more than 300 pages and 1,100 terms—but that is only the beginning of the differences between the first edition and this one.

On the first page of this book, like Robinson Crusoe, I noted foot-prints, few and faint but discernible, on the terrain I was proposing to explore. As I followed the tracks of those early explorers, I found that they all led back to the same fountainhead: *The Book of St. Albans*. Though the *Egerton, Porkington, Harley, Gloucester* and *Digby* manuscripts and the printed *Hors, Shepe & the Ghoos* antedate Dame Juliana's book, it is, finally, to the village of St. Albans that every one of my predecessors pilgrimaged.

In the sixteenth century alone there were fifteen editions of *The Book of St. Albans*; a complete venereal bibliography would fill several pages (which I have omitted in the continuing conviction that this book's province is Arcadia, not Academe).

Why have Dame Juliana's one hundred sixty-four terms evoked five hundred years of often heated debate by dozens of scholars? *The Book of St. Albans* isn't, after all, the Rosetta Stone, and yet, sphinxlike, it has posed its riddle to passing travelers for five hundred years. As any reader of the first edition of this book knows, I was caught, then intrigued, then possessed by it in my turn. As the reader of *this* edition will discover, I have seized the opportunity to answer at last the questions left unanswered in the first edition of *An Exaltation of Larks*, and in all the books and treatises that preceded it; I have undertaken, in short, to solve the riddle of *The Book of St. Albans*.

That solution—and the sometimes tortuous paths that led me to it—lie ahead in the pages that follow, where the reader will find many names, Caxton, Turberville, Skinner, Osbaldiston, Daniel, Blades, Hodgkin, Hare—but special note should be made of three invaluable sources: the Oxford English Dictionary, C. E. Hare's *The Language of Field Sports*, and John Hodgkin's *Proper Terms*.

The Oxford English Dictionary is referred to in these pages as the OED, and occasionally as the NED, which stands for New English Dictionary, though in fact the NED is older than the OED. The "New" in New English Dictionary arose out of the Philological Society's dissatisfaction in 1857 with all the English language dictionaries that preceded their resolve to make a new and definitive one. In 1879, James A. H. Murray, a master at Mill Hill School, who had emerged as the *de facto* editor of the uncompleted and continually escalating enterprise, reported to the Philological Society that he had "commenced the erection of an iron building, detached from my dwelling-house, to serve as a *Scriptorium* . . . fitted with blocks of pigeon-holes, 1,029 in number, for the reception of the alphabetically arranged slips" from sub-editors scattered all over Britain and beyond, a subsequent record reporting that "the letter H came . . . all the way from Florence." Thus was begun a magnificent labor that became the Oxford English Dictionary on January 1, 1895, with the publication of the catchily-titled *Deceit to Deject* volume. The labors of the editors of the OED resemble those of Sisyphus, the *Académie Française*, and bridge-painters, who live out their lives on the span, reaching one end of the Golden Gate or George Washington only to return and begin again at the other which has faded and eroded (as have, presumably, the painters) in the years consumed by their one-way trip. So too, when the OED philologists arrive finally at Z, there is just time for a cup of tea, then back to A.

The result of this unending devotion is a work of such scope and authority that no writer who presumes to examine the English language can do without it, as the following pages will attest.

C. E. Hare's *Language of Field Sports* is one of two major twentieth century assaults on *The Book of St. Albans*. In its Second Edition, published in 1948, Hare translated most of Dame Juliana's hunting terms, but nimbly sidestepped the fanciful terms with, "The derivation of all the group terms for persons (and objects) form as fascinating a study as those for animals and birds. The notes, however, would be too long for insertion in this work."

My research for the first edition of *An Exaltation of Larks* led me to Hare's admirable book; and his frequent reference to, and evident reliance on, *Proper Terms* by John Hodgkin sent me in pursuit of that book, published in England in 1909 in an edition of only one hundred copies, with the subtitles SUPPLEMENT TO THE TRANSACTIONS OF THE PHILOLOGICAL SOCIETY, 1907–1910, and AN ATTEMPT AT A RATIONAL EXPLANATION OF THE COLLECTION OF PHRASES IN "THE BOOK OF ST. ALBANS," 1486, ENTITLED "COMPAYNYS OF BEESTYS AND FOWLYS," AND SIMILAR LISTS.

Note Hodgkin's cautious "attempt" and "*rational* explanation." Here, clearly, was a scholar who understood—and shared—my dilemma, and had apparently written the definitive work on the subject. My search for the book was fruitless, and finally my deadline dictated that *An Exaltation of Larks* would leave the dock without Hodgkin's precious charts and advisories.

Twenty-two years later, when destiny placed another chance in my hands, I resolved to cast a last net for one of the one hundred copies (now nearly a century old!) of John Hodgkin's *Proper Terms*.

The work on this edition proceeded, the new deadline neared, the author despaired . . . and then one day, a librarian in the Research Department of the New York Public Library (let posterity note that his name is Peter McDonald) informed me that he thought he had located a copy, the only one in the United States, in the Wilson Library of the University of Minnesota.

A prayerful call to the Wilson Library located a librarian in Inform who confirmed the good news that John Hodgkin's *Proper Terms* was listed in the library's catalogue. Then came the bad news: it couldn't be found: in the years since anyone had inquired about it it seemed to have disappeared. The next day, good news: it wasn't on the Lost Books list. Better news: it would be included in the next Search. Best news: the next scheduled Search was slated for tomorrow! Two days later, calamitous news: the book had failed to turn up in a thorough search of the stacks, and the next Search would exceed the limits of my deadline.

As the prize shimmered just beyond my fingertips, vanished, reappeared, then vanished again, my spirits soared or sank with each call, so conspicuously with the last that the Wilson librarian asked why the book was of such importance to me, and I explained my twenty-two year quest. Silence, then the librarian said he might come back to the library tonight to conduct his own search; books had, he said, a way of migrating. That evening there was a call, and a voice asking, "Does a sounder of swine sound familiar?" Let posterity note and angels record that the voice belonged to Robert Ash, and that, like the surprise witness who shows up at the last instant in a courtroom drama, Hodgkin arrived on my doorstep the next morning, with 187 closely-printed, closely-reasoned pages that provided the final pieces in the puzzle that had taunted me for twenty-two years, and my philological betters for five hundred. In the Ultimate Edition of *An Exaltation of Larks*, the venereal list is complete.

The terms that follow are authentic and authoritative. They were used, they were correct, and they are useful, correct—and available—today.

A MURDER OF CROWS

The term appears in the oldest of the manuscripts, Egerton, *as* a Mursher of Crowys. *By 1476 it had become the more easily recognizable* Murther of Crowes *in* The Hors, Shepe & the Ghoos.

AN UNKINDNESS OF RAVENS
From the legend that ravens pushed their young from the nest to be "nourished with dew from heaven," as The Folk Lore of British Birds *put it in 1885, until the adult birds "saw what colour they would be."*

A FALL OF WOODCOCK
In the Harleian Miscellany, *Charles Morton quoted Scripture,* Jeremiah viii:7, " *'Yea, the Stork in the heaven knoweth her appointed times; and the turtle and the crane, and the swallow observe the time of their coming.' " Morton went on, "Consider their coming, which is so sudden . . . that it is as if they dropped in upon us from above. In woodcocks especially it is remarkable that upon a change of the wind to the east, about Alhallows-tide, they will seem to have come all in a night; for though the former day none are to be found, yet the next morning they will be found in every bush . . ." "This sudden appearance of the birds is what is meant by* 'a ffalle of Woodecockys,' " *says* Hodgkin in Proper Terms, *"and the phenomenon is metaphorically comparable to a* fall *of snow." Parenthetically, we discover in Jeremiah viii that the swallows' return to Capistrano was foretold in the Old Testament!*

A DULE OF DOVES
A corruption of the French deuil, *mourning. The soft, sad ululation of the dove has always evoked the sense of mourning. The fifteenth century* Porkington MS *offers* a pitying of turtyllys *(turtledoves; see the next term).*

A TRUE LOVE OF TURTLEDOVES

Doves appear variously in the lists of venery as doves and turtledoves. Where they are not sad they are faithful. The second Harley Manuscript *has a* Trewloufe of Turtyllys, *and the* Robert of Gloucester MS *has* A Trewloue of Turtuldowys. *When Shakespeare's Troilus commends his love to Cressida, he compares it (favorably) to lovers' customary clichés, "truth tired with iteration: as true as steel, as plantage to the moon, as sun to day,* as turtle to her mate . . ." *A scant hundred years after* The Book of St. Albans, *the turtledove's fidelity was "truth tired with iteration."*

A CLOWDER OF CATS

The second Harley MS *lists* a clowdyr of carlys, *as do the* Robert of Gloucester *and* Digby Manuscripts, *since, in the north of England, tom-cats were called carl-cats. In 1450, under* a Cloudyr of Cattys, The Egerton Manuscript *warned sternly,* "non dicitur *a clouster" (One doesn't say 'a cluster').*

A CLUSTER OF HOUSECATS
No sooner proscribed than done. In 1476, The Hors, Shepe & the Ghoos *defiantly listed* a Cluster of tame cattes.

A CLUTTER OF CATS
Hodgkin weighs in with the opinion that clowder "is probably the same word as clutter, *and is evidently the proper term to be used for 'a lot of cats.' " Lest the matter—and the harried cats—rest there, the first* Harley MS *insists on* a Gloryng of Cattis, *for which, Hodgkin says, "The Pr. Parv. gives* 'GLARYN *or bryghtly shynyn':* [glaring] *is evidently the proper term to use of a cat's eyes shining in the dark."*

A DESTRUCTION OF WILDCATS
The Porkington MS *enters the lists with* a Dovt of Wyld cattys. Dovt *translates to* Do-out, *which meant* destruction, *as noted in* The Hors, Shepe & the Ghoos's a destruction of wild cattes.

A KINDLE OF KITTENS
Kin, kindred, *and the German* Kinder *are related to this word from the ME* kindlen. *To* kindle *means literally "to give birth." The term appears in* The Book of St. Albans *as* A Kyndyll of yong Cattis.

A KENNEL OF DOGS
A Kenell of Rachis *in* The Book of St. Albans. *The OED traces* rache *to the Old Norman* rakki, *dog, and suggests this term be used for a pack "of dogs of any kind." So be it.*

A MUTE OF HOUNDS
In Old French, meute *meant either* pack *or* kennel. *Though this is the term found most often in the old lists, I am partial to the occasionally encountered* sleuth of hounds, *(from the Icelandic word for "trail").*

A LEASH OF GREYHOUNDS
Also a brace.

A COUPLE OF SPANIELS
In The Book of Hunting, *1575, George Turberville explained it all, more or less: "As of Greyhounds two make a* Brase, *and of hounds a* couple. *Of Greyhounds three make a* Lease [*leash*], *and of hounds a* Couple and a halfe. *We let slippe a Greyhoŭd, and we cast off a hound. The string wherewith we leade a Greyhound is called a* Lease, *and for a hound a* Lyame . . . *Many other differences there be, but these are most vsuall [*usual*]." In the unlikely event any more information is wanted, a* liam *was the silk or leather rope by which hounds were held.*

A COWARDICE OF CURS

A Cowardnes of curris *is the 117th term in* The Book of St. Albans.

A MURMURATION OF STARLINGS

An old and honorable term that appears as a Murmuracion of stares, *or a close variant of that spelling, in all the early manuscripts and books.*

A CHATTERING OF CHOUGHS

The twenty-seventh term in The Book of St. Albans *list. The* Egerton MS *has* Claterying. *The chough is a red-legged bird related to the crow.*

A SPRING OF TEAL

The birds' action when flushed. Since these were hunting terms, the behavioral characteristic of the birds and animals when fleeing was of critical importance. In the 1632 edition of Six Court Comedies, *published by Edward Blount, the subject comes up in a play called* Mydas *when Petulus says that someone "hath . . . started a covey of Bucks or roused a school of Pheasants."*

HUNTSMAN: *Treason to two brave sports, hawking and hunting! Thou shoudst say, "Start* a hare, rouse the deer, spring the partridge."

PETULUS: *I'll warrant that was devised by some Country swad [bumpkin] that seeing a hare skip up, which made him start, he presently said he started the hare.*

LICIO: *Aye, and some lubber lying besides a spring and seeing a partridge come by, said he did spring the partridge.*

HUNTSMAN: *Well remember all this.*

PETULUS: *Remember all? Nay then we had good memories, for there be more phrases than thou hast hairs.*

A BARREN OF MULES

The Egerton MS *has* Burdynne of Mulyse. *Hodgkin poses the possibility "that* barren *or* baren [*which appear in most of the other sources, including* The Book of St. Albans] *may be a corruption of the word* berynge [*bearing*], *with a* double entendre, *suggested by the* barrenness of mules." *Since 500 years of exegesis have resulted in a standoff, and since the fifteenth century scribes and printers often omitted the final* g, *and* barren *allows for both* barren *and* bearing—*I propose that the reader render the final verdict.*

A PASS OF ASSES

In the first edition of this book, I linked The Book of St. Albans's Pase of Assis *to the Latin* passus, *a step or stride, and therefore translated* pase *as* pace, *as had most of the early authorities and the OED. But in the years since the publication of* An Exaltation of Larks *I have encountered other opinions. In considering* pace of asses *and* rag of colts, *Hodgkin sighs, "There has been more trouble arriving at what appears to me to be the true and satisfactory explanation of this pair of terms than with any other in the series." Examining Wright's 1857* Vocabularies, *Hodgkin says, "Apparently he has suggested the word 'step' as an easy translation for* passus. *But this is not what it means." He notes that "the St. Albans printer, followed by Wynkyn de Worde, drops an* s *and makes* [*the Egerton MS's* passe] pase, *probably not knowing what it meant. Subsequently* [*various authorities*] *and the N.É.D.* [*OED*] *all turn this into* pace, *thus completely losing sight of the fact that the word was originally* passe." *Mea culpa! Hodgkin's conclusion is that both* pace *and* rag "*refer to the 'track' or 'walk' of these particular quadrupeds to their feeding grounds, or elsewhere . . . The interpretations which suggested themselves as* pace . . . *will not do now that the fifteenth century Nominale expression is in evidence, and the Egerton MS List clearly shows that the word for 'asses' was* passe, *not* pace *as we understand it." Pace Hodgkin, "pace" is scrapped, and the euphonious* pass of asses *it will be, now and forever, time without end, amen.*

A HARRAS OF HORSES

Hara *in Latin meant a pigsty, hence any enclosure for animals. In French,* haras *means stud-farm.*

A RAG OF COLTS
There has been considerable conjecture about this term. It may be related to rage, *a word we will encounter later in another context; it may derive from the Old Norse* rögg *(whence "rug"), signifying something shaggy (like a colt's coat). Hare conjectures that it is the word that became our word "rack," one of the gaits of a five-gaited horse. Hodgkin is firm, insisting that this term, via* rack, *expresses "the same meaning as the word* passe *used in connection with* asses [q.v., above]."

A STUD OF MARES
In orthography and meaning, stud *has changed little in 500 years. Stud descends via* stod *from the Old English* standan, *to stand. To this day, wherever a stallion is available as a sire, he is said to be "standing," and does, in word and deed, "stand" over a mare.*

AN OSTENTATION OF PEACOCKS

The Book of St. Albans *has* muster of peacocks, *which the OED says Dame Juliana copied from* The Hors, Shepe & The Ghoos, *in the sense of "show, display," the OED's first definition of* muster. *The original use of the word had much more the sense of* proud display *than its later (and current) use as a military term:* A MUSTER OF SOLDIERS, *for inspection. It is in* The Illustrated Sporting and Dramatic News *that* ostentation of peacocks *makes its first appearance, in 1925. Perhaps the periodical's Drama Department overruled the Sporting experts to restore to the peacock the colorful and descriptive term that more closely reflects the fifteenth century definition of the word "muster."*

A HILL OF RUFFS
The ruff is the male of a bird of the sandpiper family, of which the female is a reeve. In Rural Sports, 1801, *the Rev. Mr. W. B. Daniel writes that "soon after their arrival, the Ruffs begin to* hill, *that is . . . collect on some dry bank . . . in expectation of the Reeves, which resort to them."*

A GANG OF ELK

Elk appear in the text, but not the venereal list, of the Book of St. Albans. Gang of elk *appears in W. Irving's* Astoria: *"They saw . . . frequent gangs of stately elks."*

A HERD OF HARTS

The now commonplace herd *is one of the most frequently used terms in the early manuscripts and books, showing up to describe* harts, hinds, bucks, curlew, and even, *in one of Dame Juliana's waggish moments,* harlots *(q.v.). In the fifteenth century there were in fact so many uses for* herd *that Dame Juliana finally threw up her hands with the portmanteau* an herde of all mañ (manner of) deer.

A BEVY OF ROEBUCKS

See earlier note on BEVY OF BEAUTIES. *When applied to roes there would seem to be some support for the argument that it stems from the French word for drinking, since roes would be seen together at a watering place.*

A COLONY OF RABBITS

A HUSK OF HARE
Also sometimes a down of hare. *Neither* husk *nor* down *has been tracked to its lair. Of* husk, *Hodgkin says,* "*nothing can be said with certainty—Dr. Bradley suspects some scribal error, which the later lists have copied . . .* Downe *suggests comparison with the word* donie, *a hare.*" *The* Egerton MS *offers* drove of hare *from the manner in which they were sometimes hunted.*

A DRAY OF SQUIRRELS
"*In the summer time they build them nests (which in our countrey are called* Drayes*)*"—*Topsell's* History of Foure-footed Beastes, *1607.*

A SORDE OF MALLARDS

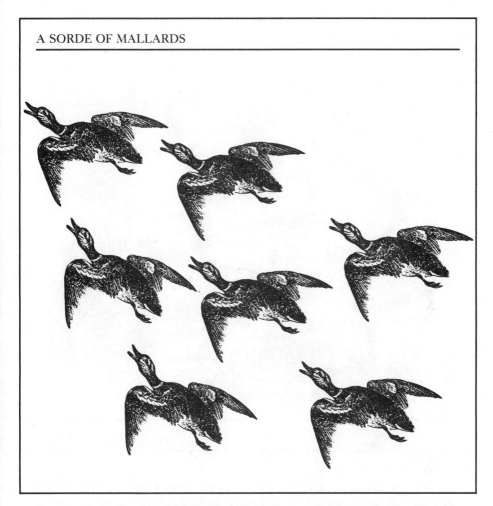

Egerton *has* a ff025lushe of Mallardys; St. Albans et al *have* a Sorde. *Hodgkin observes, "The mallard is the male wild duck, and the term* ff025lushe *is onomatopoetic, and is so called from the manner in which they rise from the water [see the note on* route of wolves].*" But the term generally used in connection with mallards is* sort, sorde, sourde, *from the Latin* surgere, *to rise.*

A PADDLING OF DUCKS
On water. In Conan Doyle's Sir Nigel, *the Knight of Duplin insists on* badling, *which he has apparently taken from* The Book of St. Albans' badelyng of Dokis. *However, the earlier Egerton Manuscript has a* Padelynge of Dookysse, *which looks and sounds like what Dame Juliana meant to say—or write, so I elect to go with* Egerton *over* St. Albans *and the crusty knight.*

A TEAM OF DUCKS
In the air. The Anglo Saxon word team *meant* offspring. *The word* teeming *derives from it, and so does the proper term for ducks in flight.*

A GAGGLE OF GEESE *on water*

A SKEIN OF GEESE *in flight*

A COVER OF COOTS

A Couert of cootis, *as the term appears in all the early lists, is derived from* couvert, *the past participle of the French verb* couvrir, *to cover or conceal, so we have the choice of* cover *or* covert *of coots. Since the coot's nest is notoriously jerry-built and poorly concealed,* cover *(over the eggs), not* covert *(well hidden), is what seems to have been meant.*

A RAFTER OF TURKEYS

Probably not what you think, if you see birds sitting on a beam. The term is related to raft *in the sense of "a large and often motley collection of people and things, as a* raft *of books," according to Webster. It is also related to* raff, *which means a collection of things, and appears in some interesting variations in* riffraff *and* raffish. *Remember* raff, *we will encounter it again.*

A DRIFT OF HOGS

A Dryft of tame swyne *in* The Book of St. Albans. *In Thomas Wright's* Volume of Vocabularies, *1857,* drift *is defined as a driving of beasts.*

A SOUNDER OF SWINE

This is one of those words that suffered some interesting sea-changes hopping back and forth across the English Channel. Originally it was the Old English word sunor, *meaning herd. The Normans adopted it and it became Gallicized to* soundre. *Since Norman French was the language of all the earliest hunting treatises, and thus the principal source of hunting terms, the word returned to England as* sounder, *with the English none the wiser that they were borrowing back their own rake. The hunting word "redingote" made a similar trip. The snobbish French affected the English word "riding-coat" which, in their accent, became red-in-goat. The snobbish English, affecting French, heard the word, thought it French, and took it back across the Channel as redingote, which it has remained to this day.*

A DROVE OF CATTLE
The Book of St. Albans: a Droue of nete [*the Old English word for an ox or bullock, cow or heifer*].

A TRIP OF GOATS
A very widely used term, given by eighteen authorities. It could come from the Icelandic thrypa, *meaning "flock," or it could be a corruption of "tribe." The fifteenth century's orthographic ingenuity is demonstrated by the wild variety of spellings of "goat" in the lists: gete, geete, gayte, goete, gotes, geates, etc.*

A SKULK OF FOXES

A COVEY OF PARTRIDGE

Here is an interesting etymological journey: the Latin cubare *means "to lie down" (both* concubine, *to lie down* with, *and* incubate, *to lie down* on, *also derive from this root). It becomes* cover *in Old French, whence* cove *or* covy *in Middle English. Thus it refers to nesting habits.*

A HOST OF SPARROWS
Hodgkin, who is grudging about many of the terms, salutes Dame Juliana's Ost of sparowis *as a true "company term . . . There is the notion of an army or hostile force [see the note on* host of angels], *and not without cause, from their destructive habits."*

A DESCENT OF WOODPECKERS
The NED or New English Dictionary, *which is in fact the old English Dictionary, renamed the* Oxford English Dictionary *in 1895, gave* descent *as "the alleged term for a flight of* woodwales" *or green woodpeckers which do in fact swoop down. This term appears only in* The Hors, Shepe & the Ghoos, *next to* an Exaltation of Larkes.

A LEAP OF LEOPARDS

Egerton, Porkington, The Hors, Shepe & the Ghoos, *and* The Book of St. Albans *all include, in various spellings*, a Lepe of Lebardis: *surprising until one remembers that, when Nigel responded to a demand that he name a group of lions, "I am not like to meet several lions in Woolmer Forest," the Knight of Duplin replied, "Who can tell how far afield such a knight errant as Nigel of Tilford may go, when he sees worship to be won." These lists were intended to be comprehensive, as* leap of leopards, pride of lions *and* shrewdness of apes *attest*.

A CRASH OF RHINOCEROSES
The term is in contemporary use in the Kenya Game Reports.

A SLOTH OF BEARS
When Dame Juliana wrote a Sleuth of beer *is in* The Book of St. Albans, *she opened the door to a host of errors. Following doggedly in her footsteps, generations of compilers confused her* sleuth *with the* sleuth *in a sleuth of hounds (q.v.). The "Lover of the Arts" who revised the ninth edition of Dr. John Bulloker's* English Expositor, *1695, attached the term to a "company of wild boars." In 1611, George Turberville got it right again: Not* sleuth of bears, *but "a Slowth of Beares. They are so heauie that when they be hunted they can make no speed but are alwaies within sight of the Dogges . . . when they wallow then they go at most ease."*

A MOB OF KANGAROO
Sometimes troop.

A SINGULAR OF BOARS

What have we here? Singular *to designate a group of anything? Absolutely not, Hodgkin says, quoting a poem from* The Book of St. Albans: *"And when he is of .iiij yere a beore shell he be . . . And when he is four, a bore shall he be./From the sounder of swine then departeth he./A Singular is he so: for alone he will go." Referring to Stephen Skinner's* Etymologicon Linguae Anglicanae, *1671, a work entirely in Latin that was, until Hodgkin's* Proper Terms, *the most comprehensive examination of the venereal lists, Hodgkin concludes that, in Skinner,* "synguler *is correctly explained . . . [the term] indicates solely one wild boar of four years and upwards in age, and does not apply to any greater number. George Turberville* [The Book of Hunting, 1575]," *Hodgkin continues, "curiously enough derives the word from the French* sanglier, *and says that the English word is a corruption from this, evidently not being aware of the etymology of the French word, which is unquestionably from* singularis."

If Hodgkin and Skinner are right about singular, *how do we explain the fact that twelve lists include* a singular *of boorys, borys, boores, bores—all of them unmistakably plural? Turberville was hardly being reckless in assuming* singular *sprang, as did the venereal lists, from the French.* Sanglier *is the French word for "boar," which was, in its turn, a French transliteration of the Latin word for "boar,"* singularis porcus, *as Mr. Hodgkin goes to some pains to remind us, and* singularis porcus *certainly implies that the boar travels alone, hence needs, and deserves, no group term. Game, set and match to Mr. Hodgkin . . . until one recalls that in Latin, as in English, the word "singular" means both "solitary" and "extraordinary," whereas the exclusive sense of "solitary" or "single" was usually consigned in Latin not to* singularis *but to* singulus. *A single look at the illustration on this page unravels the riddle. Hodgkin to the contrary notwithstanding,* singularis, sanglier *and* singular *all mean "extraordinary."*

A CAST OF HAWKS

The birds were "cast off" the hawker's arm.

A LEASH OF MERLINS
As noted earlier, these hawks were "for a lady," and, like the greyhound (noted earlier), they were leashed.

A FLIGHT OF GOSHAWKS
As the term informs us, these hawks were not "cast off," they were "lett fli."
Cormorants were also "lett fli": a fflyt of cormeravnttys, The Porkington Manuscript.

A CONVOCATION OF EAGLES
A term of more recent vintage, appearing for the first time in 1925, in The Illustrated Sporting and Dramatic News.

A TIDINGS OF MAGPIES

Hodgkin refers to this term as "sadly mangled," appearing as Tythiñgys *in* Porkington, Tygendis *in the 1496* St. Albans *reprint, and* Titengis *in the 1486* St. Albans. *"This strange looking word . . . is nothing more nor less than our current word tiding, or tidings," says Hodgkin, concluding, "The word means exactly what the Egerton MS. says, 'a Tydinge of Pyys' "—tidings because of the superstition that the future, for good or ill, was foretold by the number of magpies one chanced to see.*

A FLIGHT OF SWALLOWS

A MUTATION OF THRUSHES
A Mutacyoñ of threstyllys *in the* Porkington MS. *On June 1, 1867, a letter from William Dodgson in* Science Gossip *provided the "recognized fact amongst naturalists that thrushes acquire new legs, and cast the old ones when about ten years old."*

A BUILDING OF ROOKS

Hodgkin observes that rooks "make such a fuss over [their nests] that it is perhaps their most prominent characteristic, and the term is only given so that the 'yonge gentylman' shall not speak of rooks nesting. That this theory is correct," Hodgkin writes, "is borne out by 'The Book of St. Albans,' 1486 . . . On the first page of 'The Boke of Hawkynge' it states: 'And we shall say that hawkys doon draw when they bere [bear] tymbering to their nests and nott they beld ne make [not they "build or make"] their nestes.' "

A WATCH OF NIGHTINGALES
In The Folk Lore and Provincial Names of British Birds, *1885, the Rev. Charles Swainson retells the legend of the nightingale and the blindworm who had only one eye apiece. Invited to the wren's wedding, the nightingale "was ashamed to show herself in such a condition," so she stole an eye from the sleeping snake, who swore to get it back when the nightingale slept—which explains why, from that day to this, the bird has maintained a nocturnal* watch, *keeping itself awake—and us enchanted—by singing through the night.*

A CONGREGATION OF PLOVERS
As noted earlier, there are two congregations in the early lists: plovers and people. Why plovers—or people—should have been so honored is lost in the mists of time.

A NYE OF PHEASANTS

Egerton *gives us a* ny *of pheasants and* St. Albans *a* nye, *as does the Knight of Duplin. An article in* The Illustrated Sporting and Dramatic News *argues that the term "is almost certainly incorrect in the form in which the old books give it. It should not be* A Nye *but* An Eye, Eye *being an Old English word [for] a brood." All the authorities agree that* nye *in any of its forms refers only to the young of the genus, excluding the adults—which led me to opt in the first edition of this book for the fanciful but general term* bouquet *which can be found only in a 1927 compilation by Philip and Helen Gosse. In this ultimate edition I have yielded at last to the knight.*

A CHARM OF FINCHES

There is much more to this charming term than meets the eye. It appears to belong, uniquely, to three *venereal families: Onomatopoeia, Error and Comment. All the authorities agree that, as used here,* charm *is a variant of the Old English* cirm, *which meant, along with such other variants as* cherme *and* chirp, *"Noise, din, chatter, vocal noise (in later times esp. of birds)," according to the OED, which offers as illustration, "A company or flock (of finches) 1486 Bk. St. Albans F vj, A Cherme of Goldefynches." Well, there it is,* charm *meaning not a "magic spell . . . [or] quality exciting love or admiration," which is the OED's sb.[1] definition of* charm, *but an unpleasant din!* Charm, *it seems is Onomatopoetic—and the result of Error in transcription over the centuries. Disappointing. But wait. The OED wavers with "cf. also* Charm sb.[2]." *Back we hurry, from the noisy, uncharming* chirm *to the more promising precinct of* charm sb.[2]—*and, behold: "A dialectical variant of* cherme, *a common 16th c. form of* chirm. *Perhaps some fancied association with* Charm sb.[1] [*magic spell . . . exciting love*] *may have contributed to give this form its literary standing." "Noise" has given way to "enchantment," and we are back where I had hoped we would be, with a* charm *of finches in the fifth family of venereal terms: Comment—and a comment as pleasant as the term.*

A PARTY OF JAYS

The family's Latin name explains everything: Garrulus glandarius.

A DISSIMULATION OF BIRDS
From the gallant behavior of the adult birds, simulating injury to draw strangers away from the nest. In The Folklore and Provincial Names of British Birds, *1885, the Rev.* Charles Swainson *wrote, "During the season of incubation the cock bird tries to draw pursuers from the nest by wheeling round them, crying and screaming . . . whilst the female sits close on the nest till disturbed, when she runs off, feigning lameness, or flaps about near the ground as if she had a broken wing." See the next term.*

A DECEIT OF LAPWINGS
The Egerton MS *gave the correct* Dyssayte *[deceit] of* Lepwynkys, *which, like* dissimulation of birds, *refers to the adult lapwing's effort to draw an unwelcome visitor from the nest. In a rare departure from form, Dame Juliana got it wrong in* The Book of St. Albans, *where she recorded a* Desserte of Lapwynges, *which gave rise to centuries of misunderstanding. Hodgkin says testily, "The word is simply* DECEIT *and nothing else." "Far from his nest the lapwing screams away," Shakespeare wrote in* The Comedy of Errors. *In* The Assembly of Fowls, *Chaucer referred to "the false Lapwing, ful of trecherie," so there was no excuse for Dame Juliana's blunder. Finally, in a note on fifteenth century humor, Hodgkin observes that "one of the French country terms for a lapwing is* dix-huit, *from its note or cry. Perhaps," he says, "the English word 'deceit' is intended as a double entendre, or in a punning sense."*

A SIEGE OF HERONS

The Egerton Manuscript *lists together* A Sege of Betowrys [bitterns], A Sege of Hayrynnys, a Sege vnto a Castelle, *to which Hodgkin adds,* "Just as a commander lays siege to a 'castelle' . . . so does the patient heron stand at the waterside, waiting for the unwary fish to pass by"—*and therein lies a clue to one of Hamlet's more mysterious utterances,* "I am but mad north-northwest; when the wind is southerly, I know a hawk from a handsaw." *By Shakespeare's time the common tongue that had turned* "Route du Roi" *into* "Rotten Row" *had corrupted the insulting* "He doesn't know a hawk from a heronshaw (heron)" *to* "He doesn't know a hawk from a handsaw"—*a mark of churlish ignorance of the language of hunting, as the Knight of Duplin would be the first to point out. Since herons fly with the wind, a southerly wind makes them easy to distinguish by putting the hunter's back to the sun; hence Hamlet's cryptic hint to his childhood friends Rosencrantz and Guildenstern that his madness is feigned.*

A LABOR OF MOLES

The term is half a millenium old: Egerton *has* a Labyr of Mollys, The Book of St. Albans a Labor of Mollis.

A BUSINESS OF FERRETS
Like moles, found in both Egerton *and* St. Albans.

A CETE OF BADGERS
Another obscure term. Hare makes the interesting guess that it may be the Chaucerian word for "city." In the OED, the word is found among the multifarious uses of set: *"A badger's earth or warren is properly and generally called a 'set' or 'cete.' " A reader of the first edition of this book has suggested that* cete *might be a copyist's erroneous transcription of* cote, *an Anglo-Saxon word with several meanings in Middle English, one of them* chamber. *The root word survives today in* dovecote *and* cottage—*and badgers do live in underground chambers. The nod to the OED.*

A RICHNESS OF MARTENS
In 1607, Topsell, in his Foure-footed Beastes, *noted that "euery skinne [is] woorthe a French crowne or foure shillinges at the least." The marten's skin was so prized that tenth century Welsh law decreed, "Three furs which the queen is entitled to: the skin of a marten, of a beaver, and an ermine." Under* martens, *Hodgkin observes acidly, "Note Aalde's [Edward Aalde,* The Book of Hawking, Huntyng, *etc., 1586] curious misprint, 'a Riches of* Matrons,' *which was followed by Helme. This shows how little the meanings of the phrases were grasped." It also shows how seriously the game of venery has always been played, with no prisoners taken.*

A MUSTERING OF STORKS

See the note on peacocks. This is doubtless the military sense of muster, *since storks migrate in large groups, arriving and leaving in formation.*

A DOPPING OF SHELDRAKES

This term from the Harley MS *was tracked down by Hodgkin who found it in East Anglia meaning "a short quick curtsey," which Hodgkin finds appropriate to the bird's "sudden disappearance under water when disturbed."*

A SHREWDNESS OF APES

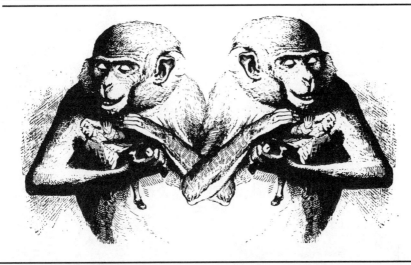

Shrewdness? *Over the centuries, the word* shrewd *has lost its original Middle-English connotation of "depraved" or "wicked," which evolved first to "mischievous" and finally to the benign cleverness it connotes today. The OED quotes Chaucer as provenance for* shrewdness *as "wickedness," and under "Naughtiness, mischieviousness" offers our premise as conclusion:* "Bk St. Albans *and* Egerton MS . . . *term for a 'company' of apes." So, we accept our own term as proof that it was in the sense of naughtiness and mischievousness that a* Shrewdenes of apis *was coined five hundred years ago. Like a homerun hitter, we've circled the bases to come back to home plate—where we started—but with a run scored.*

A ROUTE OF WOLVES

In 1658, a source identified by Hodgkin as Cowell wrote in Interpreter, *"Rout (routa) is a French word signifying a company or flock . . . It signifieth in our Common law, an Assembly of three persons or more, going on about forcibly to commit an unlawfull act, but yet do it not."*

Now that we have encountered herd, bevy, sounder *and* route, *the moment has come for a five hundred year old message from Dame Juliana in* The Book of St. Albans:

> *My chylde callith herdys of hert and of hynde*
> *And of Bucke and of Doo [Doe] where yo hem finde*
> *And a Beue [Bevy] of Roos what place they be in*
> *And a Sounder ye shall of the wylde swyne*
> *And a Rowte of wolues where they passin inne*
> *So shall ye hem call as many as they bene.*

Armed with a mnemonic device like that, the reader is ready to face the Knight of Duplin.

A SWARM OF EELS

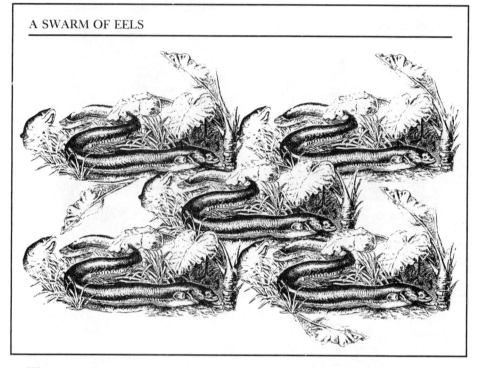

The term's first appearance is in 1801, in Rural Sports, *by the Rev. W. B. Daniel.*

AN ARMY OF HERRING
Daniel, Rural Sports, *op. cit.*

A QUANTITY OF SMELT
This entry is memorable not for the colorless term of venery conferred on the fish two hundred years ago by the busy Rev. Mr. Daniel but for the aromatic name of the fish itself. As the poker-faced parson points out, "the Germans distinguish it by the very elegant title of the Stinckfish.*"*

A SHOAL OF BASS

A HOVER OF TROUT

A BALE OF TURTLES
To my knowledge no one has ever successfully tracked this term to its lair. C. E. Hare suspects that it may be one of the erroneous terms, a corruption of dule, *since early scribes sometimes confused turtledoves with turtles. The reader who tried to decipher* cete *suggested that* bale *might be descended from the Old French* baillier, *which he translates as* to shut in *or* confine, *as the shell does the turtle, but in modern French* bailler *means* to gape, *so the term's origin remains as well concealed as the turtle.*

A GAM OF WHALES

A whaling voyage could last as long as three years, so when two whalers encountered each other on some remote sea, it called for a gam, *an exchange of crews via whaleboats and the "gamming chair." It was a happy time for a whaleman and, obviously, the whales' habit of sporting playfully on the surface of the sea gave rise to this fanciful term.*

A SCHOOL OF PORPOISES

A POD OF SEALS
The reference to peas in a pod is obvious. Pod *was applied by sailors to seals, and small groups of whales.*

A SMACK OF JELLYFISH

A KNOT OF TOADS

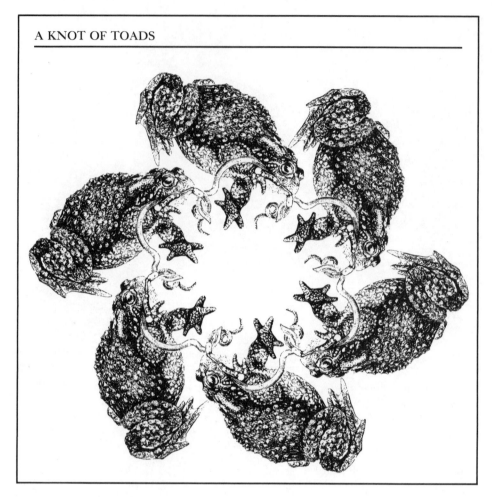

A COLONY OF FROGS

A BUSINESS OF FLIES
A Besynes of flyes *is the sixty-second term in* The Hors, Shepe, & the Ghoos, *printed by Caxton in 1476, ten years before the appearance of* The Book of St. Albans.

A FLOCK OF LICE
A Flock of lyse *is the sixty-first term in* The Hors, Shepe & the Ghoos.

A WEDGE OF SWANS

After the publication of the first edition of this book, many correspondents inquired about the omission of a term for swans. The impressive sight of a group of swans, they reasoned, couldn't have escaped the notice of the Knight of Duplin and his sporting coevals. My correspondents were correct: there is indeed a term for swans, dating from the fifteenth century and appearing in The Book of St. Albans *and numerous other sources, but its inclusion here will put to rest any questions about its omission from the first edition:* an Herde of Swannys *is a singularly colorless term for so inviting a subject. By the time the second edition of* An Exaltation of Larks *had been published, Col. R. J. Nicol's* Collection of Terms, Denoting Assemblages of Animals, Birds, Human Beings, Etc. *had provided the improved but still inadequate* wedge of swans. *We can take heart from T. S. Eliot's assertion that words "slip, slide . . . will not stay in place," which is simply to say that the swans—and the English language—await your creative contribution.*

As do, perhaps, the next four terms which, like the wedge of swans, arrived at the gangplank after the first edition of this book had sailed. Here they are, for better or worse, for your critical and by now informed judgment.

A HERD OF CRANES

An Herde of cranys *in* The Books of St. Albans, *but, like the* herd of swans, *unacceptably dull in such an imaginative list.*

A HERD OF WRENS

An Herde of Wrennys, The Book of St. Albans. *Hodgkin says, "The wren was probably allowed the term of 'herd' . . . because it was the king of birds." I say, "Regicide." I say, "Help!"*

A COLONY OF PENGUINS

A COMPANY OF PARROTS *Acceptable if* company *is a pun.*

A CRY OF PLAYERS

The proper venereal term for a troupe of actors in the sixteenth century.

A CAST OF BREAD

A cast of Brede, *as it appears in* The Book of St. Albans, *is defined in* Harrison's Description of England: *"Of the flower of one bushell they make fortie cast of manchet [fine white table-bread]."*

A CLUTCH OF EGGS

Clutch *is a Kentish variant of* cletch, *which meant a brood or hatching of chickens, and, according to the OED,* "contempt.[uously] a family."

A PEEP OF CHICKENS

A PARLIAMENT OF OWLS

A HERD OF CURLEWS
As we saw with herd of wrens, *being "herded" was an honor. Curlews are so honored in both* Egerton *and* St. Albans, *joining a select group of birds, animals and, as noted earlier, harlots.*

A WALK OF SNIPE
The observant reader will doubtless notice that I part company here with the doughty Knight of Duplin, who, in the first pages of this book, sternly instructed his student Nigel that snipe gather in a wisp. *The knight's error proves that, like great Homer, even Conan Doyle could nod—and reveal his sources.* Wisp of snipe *appears only in Osbaldiston's* British Sportsmen, *published in 1785, which means Conan Doyle could have read it (and obviously did), but the Knight of Duplin could not. The knight would have known only the* Egerton MS *and* The Book of St. Albans, *which employ* walke of snytis, *as I have, from the bird's normal manner of locomotion.*

AN EXALTATION OF LARKS

A **Exaltacyon of larkys** *is the twenty-second term in the earliest of all the lists, the* Egerton Manuscript, *1450*.

IV

The Unexpected

In Part I, I mentioned the witty, revelatory digressions into the realm of poetry by Dame Juliana, or the schoolmaster printer, or whoever wrote *The Book of St. Albans*. Now that you have read the hunting terms from her list and others', it may surprise you, as it did me, to discover that, of the one hundred sixty-four terms in *The Book of St. Albans*, seventy of them refer not to animals, but to people and life in the fifteenth century, and every one of these social terms makes the same kind of affectionate or mordant comment that the hunting terms do.

By 1486, the terms of venery were already a game, capable of codification; and if you think that the social terms were casually intended and soon forgotten, be advised that the ninth term in the *St. Albans* list is the perennial BEVY OF LADIES, and the seventeenth term in the list is none other than A CONGREGATION OF PEOPLE, a true term of venery, appearing between A WALK OF SNIPES and the eponymous EXALTATION OF LARKS. The social terms are scattered throughout the list, with nothing to distinguish them from the hunting terms. Obviously, Dame Juliana considered *all* the terms valid and of equal importance to anyone anxious to avoid the title of "churl."

As the reader will see, these social terms were the most elusive and challenging terms in the list, not just for me but for every explorer who preceded me. As noted earlier, Hare avoided them altogether, and even the redoubtable Hodgkin left a final verdict on some of them to history—and this book. Some of the social terms have given rise to linguistic free-for-alls that have endured for five hundred years (and are recorded here). Perhaps the pages that follow will put controversy to rest once and for all.

That may not occasion dancing in the streets—by anyone but me— but I think it is fair and accurate to say that, beyond the wit and imagination these social terms exhibit, they preserve the fifteenth century as if in a time capsule, providing more than a portrait of every stratum and arena of fifteenth century life: each term—SKULK, LYING, DIGNITY, SUBTLETY, RASCAL, SCOLD, FAITH—is both portrait and comment, as if, somehow, Hogarth and Dickens had been genetically combined and time-warped to the fifteenth century. Who knows, in another five hundred years, if our planet, the human race, the language and a few tattered pages of this book have survived, someone perusing the terms gathered under the rubrics People, Places & Things, or Daily Life, or Religion may gain a similar insight into the life, times, prejudices and predilections of the last decade of the twentieth century.

From this point on, a new figure appears on the venereal playing field: the nineteenth-century French lithographer Grandville (1803–1847), whose work the Encyclopædia Britannica describes as "characterized by a marvelous fertility of satirical humor." In 1968, finding Grandville's lithographs remarkably appropriate to the terms I was unearthing, I included in the first edition of *An Exaltation of Larks* as many as a frenetic search could locate. It wasn't until a dozen years later that Grandville's complete works surfaced, too late for the first edition, but in time for this one. The vast anthropomorphic world he created for periodicals like *Le Charivari* was finally at hand to make its trenchant comments on the terms of venery, as they reluctantly yielded up their five-hundred-year-old secrets.

Herewith, with pictures by Grandville, modified by Kedakai, the game of venery, as it was played in *The Book of St. Albans* in the year of our Lord 1486.

A PONTIFICALITY OF PRELATES

"An allusion," Hodgkin says, "to pope-like airs that the prelates assumed."

A SUPERFLUITY OF NUNS

The first Harley Manuscript *had a reverent* holynesse of Nunys—*but that was the last reverential note to be heard. All the lists that followed had, in one orthography or another,* a Superfluyte of Nunnys, *which Hodgkin termed "no sarcastic allusion, but the plain belief bluntly stated." Clearly, long before the birth of Henry VIII, Reformation was looming.*

AN ABOMINABLE SIGHT OF MONKS

As if this term weren't insulting enough, The Hors, Shepe & the Ghoos *has a* Lordship of monkes, *which sent Hodgkin to the NED where he found a definition of " 'lordliness, arbitrariness,' which," he remarked, "is a sufficiently good explanation."*

AN OBSERVANCE OF HERMITS

The OED defines The Book of St. Albans' Obseruans of herimytis *as "A company of religious persons observing some rule, or belonging to some order," and Hodgkin adds drily, they "were very punctilious over their observances, which are sure to have been quite sufficiently publicly performed to stimulate almsgiving."*

A DISCRETION OF PRIESTS

Referring presumably—and anxiously—to the confidentiality of the confessional. In a masterful example of British understatement, Hodgkin says of this term, "Most of the ecclesiastical terms are evidently inspired with an absence of love for the clergy."

AN UNTRUTH OF SUMMONERS

Geoffrey Chaucer's Canterbury Tales *were written precisely a hundred years before* The Book of St. Albans, *but it is in the Prologue to* The Friar's Tale *that we find the answer to the riddle the fifteenth century lists pose with their* vntrouth of Sompneris. *"I wil you of a sompnour telle a game,"* the *Friar promises his fellow guests gathered at the Tabard Inn in Southwark. "A sompnour is a renner up and doun . . . A summoner is a runner up and down/ With summonses for fornication (fornicacioun),/And is well-beat[en] at end of every town." Forming partnerships with whores, the summoner would seize them in* flagrante delicto, *"and summon to the chapter-house those two/And fleece the man and let the harlot go." So vile was a summoner's reputation, the Friar says, he "durste not for very filth and schame/Sayn that he was a sompnour, for the name."*

A SKULK OF FRIARS
Since one of the listening company at Tabard's Inn is a summoner, the even- handed Chaucer gives him the floor next, and, to no one's surprise, he elects to tell a Canterbury tale about a friar, which begins in Hell where, "Just as the bees come swarming from a hive,/Out of the Devil's arse-hole there did drive/ Full twenty thousand friars in a rout,/And through all Hell they swarmed and ran about." During the convulsive transition from Medieval to Tudor England, the battlefield was safer than the basilica; and if Pope Clement had bothered to read The Canterbury Tales—*or* The Book of St. Albans—*England might be Roman Catholic today.*

A CONVERTING OF PREACHERS

Hodgkin holds this to be "one of the sarcastic [clerical] terms." Which ones were not?

A LYING OF PARDONERS

Pardoners traveled about, selling the Pope's indulgences. Naturally, this gave rise to a bit of charlatanry. In the fifteenth century pardoners were a common sight in the stocks with their forged papal bulls tied round their necks, and in the Calendar of Letters from the Mayor and the Corporation of the City of London, 1350–1370, *there is an account of "one John Worthin, a friar, [who made himself out to be] on more intimate terms with the Holy Father at Avignon [Pope Clement IV] than any other person of the English nation."*

A SCHOOL OF CLERKS

The reference is to divinity school.

A DIGNITY OF CANONS

With clerks, canons *seem to be the only clerics to emerge from the game of venery unscathed.*

A PRUDENCE OF VICARS

The Church in England fared little better than the Roman See at the hands of Dame Juliana and her colleagues. Hodgkin's ecumenical note on this term is, "Probably intended as a sarcastic allusion to the imprudence or improvidence of vicars, e.g. large families and infinitesimal incomes and the like."

A CHARGE OF CURATES
A curate was so called because he was charged with the cura (cure) of souls, hence charge of curates. On the other hand, given the tenor of the other terms, a pun may have been intended and this term may in fact depict a regiment of clergymen charging toward a cowering clump of sinners.

A DISWORSHIP OF SCOTS
Since the Porkington MS and the two Caxton lists had stottes, this term has been the subject of fervent debate for 500 years. Hodgkin agrees with the school that associates the term with Plough Monday, when rowdy young men yoked themselves in the traces like stots (bullocks) and ploughed up the grounds of anyone who refused them refreshment or money. The Plough Monday explanation, a correspondent wrote to Chambers' Book of Days in 1863, "satisfactorily unravels the mystery of 'a disworship of Scots.'" Not quite. The venereal lists were compiled during the age of bitter wars between the English and Scots. The OED calls disworship, meaning dishonor, the "term for a company of Scots"—and so do I.

A DOCTRINE OF DOCTORS

Doctrine comes to English via 12th-century French from the Latin doctrina, *teaching. So, for that matter, does* doctor, *from* docere, *to teach, so, in this "teaching of teachers," we have a rare venereal tautology. I suppose it was inevitable.*

A SCHOOL OF SCHOLARS
Considering the Scole of scolers *in* The Hors, Shepe & the Ghoos, *the scholarly Hodgkin, who is quick to deny the legitimacy of a reputed term of venery says simply, "A company term, requiring no explanation."*

AN EXAMPLE OF MASTERS
"Schoolmasters" was meant, though, then as now, most of them probably subscribed to the philosophy of the character in Gargantua and Pantagruel *who, when criticized for not following his own advice, suggested he be thought of as "a road-sign that points the way to Paris without ever going there myself."*

AN ILLUSION OF PAINTERS

The term is Misbeleue *which, according to the OED, has more the sense of "erroneous belief" than "refusal to believe"; hence "illusion" in the sense of "trompe-l'œil." The OED also gives the term, in its original orthography, as a "term for a 'company' of painters."*

A SUBTLETY OF SERGEANTS

As the reader of these pages knows by now, each of us who has undertaken to unravel the mysteries of the venereal lists has had his bêtes noirs; this term was one of mine. Of the sergeants I have known, none were subtle, and I couldn't believe human nature had changed diametrically in a mere 500 years. So I began a slow search through dusty library stacks for the secret behind a sotelty of sergeauntis. *I found it at the end of a long list of definitions in an especially musty volume.* "Serjeant," *the book said,* "was a title borne by a lawyer." *I rest my case.*

A DAMNING OF JURORS

A Dampnyng of Jourrouris *in* The Book of St. Albans *contains the epenthetic plosive* p *that forced its unwonted, unwanted way into names like* Thompson *and words like* sompnour *(summoner)—and* dampnyng, *which tells us that* dampnyng *is damning, hence an adverse verdict.*

A SENTENCE OF JUDGES

AN ELOQUENCE OF LAWYERS

A PITY OF PRISONERS
From The Hors, Shepe, & the Ghoos.

AN EXECUTION OF OFFICERS
Term for the officers of the court who executed the court's decisions—and, in the punning (or literal) sense, the occasional hapless defendant.

A STATE OF PRINCES

A reference to their rank and precedence, which was thoroughly codified and choreographed.

A ROUTE OF KNIGHTS
Since the Nominale sive Verbale, *a manuscript that dates from about 1340, contains an extensive list of the original French terms of venery, it is used often by Hodgkin and others to validate an interpretation of the early English lists. Here, it has* Aray de Chiualers, ARRAY OF KNIGHTS, *and* Route de Es-quiers, ROUTE OF SQUIRES.

A THREATENING OF COURTIERS
Hodgkin quotes Dr. Henry Bradley's opinion that this "probably refers to the insolence characteristic of this class toward their inferiors."

A TROTH OF BARONS

The term, which appears in various sources as everything from Trought *in* Egerton *to* Thongh *in* St. Albans *and* Thought *in John Helme's 1614 list, mystified me for years. I think Hodgkin only adds to the confusion by translating it as* truth. *It is in the* Porkington Manuscript's Trothe *that the term's proper form—and meaning, as a pledge of fidelity—are unveiled. The final piece of evidence is found in the Oath of Allegiance taken by the Temporal Peers at every coronation. At the coronation of Henry VII on October 30, 1485, the Peers pledged, "I become your Liegeman of Lief and Lymme . . . I become your Liegeman of Life and Limb, and of Earthly Worship: and Faith and Truth I will bear unto You to live and die against all manner of Folks. So help me God." The young Elizabeth II heard precisely those words at her coronation in 1953.*

A RASCAL OF BOYS

Self-explanatory in the fifteenth century, self-explanatory now.

A BLUSH OF BOYS
Not only do boys, *like* gaggle, *appear twice in the* St. Albans *list, but the terms cancel each other out! The differing points of view may lend credence to the argument that the list was a compilation of other lists, rather than the unified product of a single author.*

A HOST OF MEN
See the earlier note on HOST OF ANGELS

A GAGGLE OF WOMEN
Appearing in no less than thirteen of the original lists.

A GAGGLE OF GOSSIPS
From the first Harley Manuscript. *Then, as now,* gaggle *was a popular term.*

AN IMPATIENCE OF WIVES

A MULTIPLYING OF HUSBANDS
Among its definitions of multiplying, *the OED gives "Alleged term for a 'company' of husbands, 1486,* Bk. St Albans *f vij, A Multiplieng of husbondis," but hazards no guess as to the particular sense in which the word was used by Dame Juliana. On the assumption that a good man was as hard to find five hundred years ago as now, I construe the then commonplace procreative meaning of the word, as in God's biblical ordinance, "Be fruitful and multiply."*

A BEVY OF LADIES
The OED decrees this "the proper term for a company of maidens or ladies." Since the OED is the first and last word on the English language, what are we to make of the fact that its editors used "or" which doesn't seem to allow for the possibility that a lady can be a maiden—or vice versa.

A FORESIGHT OF HOUSEKEEPERS

A DRAUGHT OF BUTLERS

In the royal household, the butler was in charge of the buttery *where the* butts
[*wooden casks*] *of wine were stored. Though* The Book of St. Albans *has a*
draught of botoleris, *bottles didn't exist when the lists were compiled, so*
butlers, *as* The Hors, Shepe & the Ghoos *has it, was definitely meant,
and* draught *referred to the butler's task of* drawing *a sample of wine, "to see
if it were . . . fit for the use of his master—and himself," Hodgkin chortles,
adding, "One of the sarcastic terms."*

A SESTER OF BREWERS
Dame Juliana's a Festre of Brweris *became a* Feest of bruers *in Wynkyn
de Worde's edition of* The Book of St. Albans, *and* Feast *it remained until
Hodgkin discovered that* both *terms had been misspelled. If Dame Juliana had
written* sester *(a measure of ale in common use among brewers), there would
have been no confusion.*

A CLUSTER OF GRAPES
Yes, a genuine term of venery, codified 500 years ago.

A CLUSTER OF CHURLS
Corroboration of Claudius's rueful comment in Hamlet *that "When sorrows
come, they come not single spies, but in battalions."*

A CLUSTER OF KNOTS

A TEMPERANCE OF COOKS

A HASTINESS OF COOKS
A conflicting opinion from The Hors, Shepe, & the Goos. *Hodgkin insists this is another of the sarcastic terms, referring to the kitchen's inertia when the diner is hungry.*

A MESS OF CARVERS
An unbrewying of Kerueris, *as Dame Juliana put it, is another of the terms that didn't make it to the earlier editions of this book for the simple reason that I couldn't penetrate it. In its long history, the OED, which contains almost every other term in* The Book of St. Albans, *wouldn't touch it either—but, according to Hodgkin, the older* NED *had a listing for* embrewing, *which bears at least a passing resemblance to* unbrewyng *(though one word would seem to be the opposite of the other). The NED referred the reader from* embrewing *to* imbruing, *and it's there that the mystery begins to unravel: the verb* imbrue *means* to stain, dirty or defile. *Hodgkin dug deeper, found "Enbrewe not the table clothe" in* The Book of Keruynge [*Carving*], *and concluded that an* unbrewyng of Kerueris *"means literally making a mess with the gravy or sauce . . . and refers to careless carvers, splashing gravy on the cloth."*

A PROVISION OF STEWARDS
The steward of the house, *as he is called in most of the lists, was the head of the domestic staff.*

AN OBEISANCE OF SERVANTS

Egerton *has* Obedyens of Seraundys, St. Albans Obeisans, *which gives us the option of* obediance *or the more submissive* obeisance. *Both words come from* obey, *the former root English, the latter French. The terms were originally French, which tips the balance toward* obeisance, *as does the fact that the OED lists the St. Albans term as the "alleged term for a company of servants" under* obeisance, *rather than* obedience. *As usual, Hodgkin takes a jaundiced view, calling this "one of the sarcastic household terms" and quoting* Matthew xxi: 30: *"I go, sir: and went not."*

A SLICE OF PANTRYMEN

For 500 years everyone has had this one wrong. I didn't even attempt it until Hodgkin arrived at my desk. A Kerff of Panteris, *Dame Juliana wrote, and, since Hodgkin was the fiercest player of the game of venery, he went for Stephen Skinner's jugular when he found that in Skinner's 1607* Etymologicon Linguae Anglicanae *he had turned* Panteris *into* panthers—*in Latin, no less! Hodgkin explains that "a panter was a servant who looked after the bread, seeing that it was properly cut and served,* pannetier *in French, and his room or office was called the* pannetrie, *anglice* pantry, *and yet Skinner talks 'learnedly' about 'Pantheras seu Pardales,' the leopard being here introduced by him apparently to show his superior knowledge," Hodgkin sniffs, as he chalks up another win.*

A SET OF USHERS

Once again we find the ubiquitous set, *but in the punning sense of* set down *or* sit. *In the fifteenth century, the usher's place was next to the door of the dining hall, on a chair from which he continually sprang to escort guests to their places, according to* rank, *with the result that the* set *of ushers hardly ever* sat. *Hodgkin, who has just accused Skinner of intellectual pretension, loftily declares this term* lucus a non lucendo [*the Latin phrase for an explanation by contraries*].

A CREDENCE OF TASTERS

Here is one of the most baffling terms in The Book of St. Albans: A Credens of Seweris, *"Seamstresses?" "A subterranean conduit for sewage?" Oddly enough, the first clue to this term came from the last place I thought to look, a contemporary edition of* Webster's Dictionary, *which gave me "Sewer, fr. OF* asseoir *to seat. A medieval household officer . . . in charge of serving the dishes at table and sometimes of seating and tasting." Hodgkin provided another piece in the puzzle with a definition of* credence *from Cotgrave's* French-English Dictionary: *"A taste or essay taken of another man's meat." Cowell, in the 1607* Interpreter, *wrote, "I have heard of an old French booke containing the officers of the King of England's Court . . . [one of] whom in Court wee now call* Sewar," *and the 1530 Palsgrave dictionary filled in the puzzle's final piece with, "I sewe at meate: je taste, and je prends l'assaye [assay, test]."*

A FAITH OF MERCHANTS

Clearly meant sarcastically. The Fishmongers' Ordinances and Skinners' Charter both prohibit the "false-packing" of goods, the fifteenth century equivalent of short-weighting. Plus ça change . . .

A TABERNACLE OF BAKERS
The law decreed that "no baker shall sell bread before his oven, but [only] in the market of his lordship the King," presumably to ensure the crown its rent. The result was that bread was sold in public stalls, called tabernacula.

A SAFEGUARD OF PORTERS
The root of porter can be either of two French words, porter, *to carry, which would point to the porters we see today, or* porte, *door, which takes us to the porters of Dame Juliana's time, who were gatekeepers, and wore, for protection against the elements, an apron, like the woman's* safeguard *or surcot identified in the 1847* Dictionary of Archaic and Provincial Words *as an outer petticoat worn by women when riding, to shield them from the dirt. Since physical protection was one of the functions of a porter in the turbulent fifteenth century, and since the compilers of these early terms of venery loved to play with—and on—words, this is almost certainly a sardonic double entendre.*

A PROUD SHOWING OF TAILORS

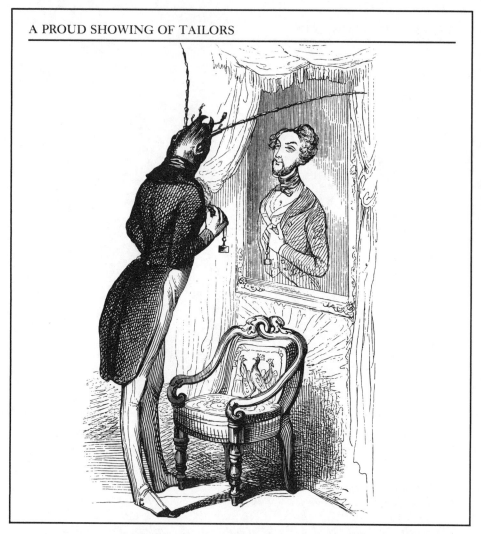

In Visions of Quevedo, *1668, J. Dodington writes, "What Lord is that* (said I) *in the Rich Clothes there, and the fine Laces? That Lord* (quoth he) *is a Taylor, in his Holy-day Clothes; and if he were now upon his Shop-board, his own Scissers and Needles would hardly know him."*

The Book of St. Albans *also has* a Disgysyng of Taylours, *in support of which Hodgkin quotes from* The Pleasant Art of Money Catching, *Glasgow, 1750, Chap. ix,* How to travel all England over without a Farthing of Money; with an Account of those that have tried the Experiment: *"He that undertakes this strange Journey, lays his first Plot how to be turned into* a brave man, *which he finds can be done by none other than a trusty* Taylor." *As a dividend, we have chanced on the 1750 edition of* Europe on Five Dollars a Day.

A SCOLD OF SEAMSTRESSES

The term in St. Albans *is a* Scoldyng of kemsteris. *This term yielded easily, but unsatisfactorily. Kempsters were female wool-combers, whom we're unlikely to encounter today. Throughout this book, where the beginning and/or ending nouns in these terms are extinct (and the term is worth preserving), I've tried to find contemporary equivalents. This term conjures up a line of overworked and bickering workers, like the cigarette girls in* Carmen, *so* seamstresses *seemed to fill the bill. Since the venereal lists were the last word in the fifteenth century. I don't think Dame Juliana would object to my effort to make them the last word in mine.*

A GORING OF BUTCHERS

A GOBBLE OF MILLERS
Dame Juliana's ffraunch of Mylneris *held even Hodgkin at bay until he "chanced to find . . . in Horman's 'Vulgaria': He is ever fraunchynge." The* OED *defines* fraunch *as "to feed greedily," and, since the Wynkyn de Worde edition of* The Book of St. Albans *refined* Mylneris *to* myllers, *Hodgkin theorizes that the miller's insatiable appetite for more corn for his mill gave rise to the elusive phrase.*

A SQUAT OF DAUBERS
The OED *gives* squat *as the proper company term for daubers, but it is unclear which "squat" is meant. There is the original meaning of "to let fall" in just the way we have seen a bricklayer flick mortar from his trowel; but fifteenth century daubers* squatted *next to a wall in order to trowel daub (of clay or cement) into it, so it seems we may take our choice.*

A LASH OF CARTERS

A WANDERING OF TINKERS
The term is double-edged. Itinerant tinkers mended household metalware, and in Scotland and Northern Ireland, gypsies—who practiced, or pretended to practice, the trade—were called tinkers, as were various "beggars, vagabonds and performers," according to the OED.

A THRAVE OF THRESHERS
Under "thresher" the OED quotes "A Thraue of Throsheris" from St. Albans, *and defines* thrave *as "Two shocks of corn." Under this term, Hodgkin makes a decisive move in the game of venery by accusing Skinner of an "extraordinary blunder" in confusing Dame Juliana's* throsshers *with* throstles, *thrushes.*

A DILIGENCE OF MESSENGERS
Any doubt that these social terms had wide currency should be dispelled by the recollection that, in more recent times, a fast coach was still called "a diligence."

Of all the professions preserved, like fossils in amber, by the venereal lists, which one would you guess appears most often? This page and the next two answer that question: shoemaking. There are no fewer than five listings for the craft in The Book of St. Albans, *which conjures up a picture of many a canny fifteenth-century youth not fortunate enough to be to the manor born waking one morning to sigh to himself, "Well, they'll always need shoes."*

A BLACKENING OF SHOEMAKERS

This term was very thorny. What Dame Juliana said was a Bleche of sowteris. *I found this singularly unilluminating, but another trek through the athenaeal dust revealed that* sowters *were shoemakers and that* bleche *meant either "bleach" or "blacken" (from the OE* blæcean*). I opted for "blacken" (it may have been the dust) and twenty-three years later was relieved to find confirmation in Hodgkin's invaluable* Proper Terms: *" 'Blecche of sowters' was a kind of ink, used at the present day, with which the soles and the heels were blackened." Explaining his odyssey on the first page of* Proper Terms, *Hodgkin speaks of "wading through the principal dictionaries, from the 'Promptorium Parvulorum' [c. 1440] upwards," and, on this term, he quotes a footnote from the Promptorium: "Wrytters ynke [writer's ink] shulde be fyner than blatche [Bleche]." I agree.*

A CUTTING OF COBBLERS

The key to this term lay at the end of a labyrinthine path, and, on the theory that the reader isn't too exhausted to make another expedition with me to the fifteenth century, I will retrace my steps. The Book of St. Albans *was printed just ten years after the date that is generally taken as the dividing line between Middle and Modern English, and, to the inexpert eye, some of these terms can appear indecipherable. Take this one: what would you make of a* Trynket of Corueseris? *Well, you would begin with* Corueseris. *The "is" you know is a fifteenth-century plural form. And you take the "u" for a "v" because until the 1820's "u" and "v" were identical. Now you have the singular "corveser," and this is where you begin in the OED, which says that "corveser" is a variant of "corviser." Very well, you move on to "corviser" and search through all the orthographic shapes it has taken through the centuries, coming finally to "corueseris, from* F. courvoisier, shoemaker." *We seem to have half our term, but why a* trynket? *Quickly enough you discover that the OED has "tryn" as a variant spelling of "trin," and then you come to the* coup de foudre. *Under "trinket" the OED says: "From the similarity of form, it has been suggested that this is the same word as Trenket, or* trynket, *a small knife, spec. a shoemaker's knife." Bingo!*

A DRUNKENNESS OF COBBLERS

The term in St. Albans *is* Dronkship. *Says the OED:* "Drunkship-DRUNK-ENNESS. *b. a drunken company 1486* Bk. of St. Albans F *vij*, a dronkship of Coblers."

A PLOCKE OF SHOETURNERS

Dame Juliana recorded a Plocke of Shoturneris, *which, by 1586 had become a* pluck of Shooturners *in Edward Aalde's* Book of Hawking, Hunting, etc. *Aalde had deciphered the second noun but not the first. 323 years later, Hodgkin solved the puzzle by finding* Pflock *in the German language, meaning a peg used by shoemakers. "Shoturners," says Hodgkin, "are clearly shoemakers who make what are known as 'turned shoes' . . . in which the shoe is made inside out and then 'turned.' "*

A SMEAR OF CURRIERS

In 1671, in his influential Etymologicon Linguae Anglicanae, *Skinner read Dame Juliana's* Smere of Coryouris *as a sweat of carriers, perceiving a group of village carriers on a hot summer day, who "multum sudorem emittunt" [emit much sweat], and Hodgkin had Skinner's hide for it—literally. "Nothing so interesting, alas!" Hodgkin huffed. "The word is* coryour, *a currier as we term it, and a smear is only the name for the chief characteristic of the currier's art": stretching the skin and smearing it "with its first black, made of Galls and Ferrailles, boil'd in . . . Sour Beer," according to* Chambers's Cyclopaedia, *1728.*

A CAJOLERY OF TAVERNERS

The vast and comprehensive Oxford English Dictionary *defines* glozing *as
"flattering, cajolery," and gives as one of its definitions, "3. An alleged name
of a 'company' (of taverners) 1486 Bk. St. Albans Fvi b, A Glosyng of
Tauerneris," which is how the term appears in the list.*

A PROMISE OF TAPSTERS
*Hodgkin explains this term as "the usual habit of tapsters . . . who say they
are 'coming now, sir,' when they have every intention of attending to . . . a
dozen other thirsty souls first." As usual, Shakespeare puts it trenchantly: "The
oath of a lover is no stronger than the word of a tapster."* As You Like It,
Act III, Sc. 4.

A LAUGHTER OF HOSTELERS
A Laughtre of Osteloris, *the proper term given in* The Book of St. Albans
*and the OED, referred to the genial bonifaces who kept the hostels and inns in
which the fifteenth century travelers stopped. Parenthetically, this note encom-
passes three discrete centuries of linguistic history, since the useful twentieth-
century word* boniface *memorializes Mr. Boniface, the innkeeper in Farquhar's*
The Beaux' Strategem, *1707.*

A MELODY OF HARPISTS
*All the terms on this and the next two pages were listed by Hodgkin under the heading "*VAGRANTS, ROGUES, MUSICIANS, ETC.*" Though the term for harpists seems benign, Hodgkin quotes* Bailey's Dictionary, *1737, on harpers "who counterfeit Blindness . . . led by a Dog or Boy." The practice was so widespread that "blind as a harper" was a common figure of speech, and "blind harper" a term of ridicule.*

A POVERTY OF PIPERS
Perhaps the pipers should have feigned blindness and taken up the harp.

A NEVERTHRIVING OF JUGGLERS
It appears that neither balls nor an instrument could beat the system. Hodgkin says jugglers came "under the category of minstrels."

AN IMPUDENCE OF PEDDLERS
The term in St Albans *is* Malepertnes. *The* OED *defines* malapert *as "Presumptuous, impudent, 'saucy.'" In Harman's* Caveat for Cursetors, *1573, we find. "These . . . Pedlars be not all evil, but . . . they are well worthy to be registered among the number of vagabonds."*

A FIGHTING OF BEGGARS

A RIFFRAFF OF KNAVES

Here is a term we have encountered before. In an earlier note I suggested that you remember raff. *The moment has come to resurrect it. This term appears in the* St. Albans *list as a* Rafull of knauys. *The OED refers you from "rayfull" or "rayful" to "raffle," and we are back to our root* raff, *obviously a popular word in the fifteenth century. This time we are told that "raffle" had as one of its meanings* riffraff, *and we have our term.*

A SKULK OF THIEVES

A GLORIFYING OF LIARS
If the crafts of advertising and P. R. had existed when The Hors, Shepe & the Ghoos *preserved a* Glorifieng of lyers, *the term's meaning would be self-evident. But since the art of glorifying by falsifying was centuries from its current flowering, we're left with the question: whom do liars glorify? Sensibly taking* glorify *in the reflexive sense, Hodgkin turned to the French language where the reflexive verb is at home, found* "Se glorifier. *To vaunt, crack, brag, boast of his owne acts, to commend or magnifie himselfe" in Cotgrave's* French-English Dictionary, *and added an acerbic, "The characteristic of this tribe."*

A HERD OF HARLOTS
"1486 Bk. St. Albans, *F vj, An Herde of harlottys," the* Oxford English Dictionary *notes solemnly among its definitions of* herd. *The Harley MS has* a haras of harlottes, *which may be a genuine confusion with* a haras of horse—or *the first gun in the barrage of* "whores" *puns eventually attributed to the Oxford dons (q. v., in the Introduction to Part V).*

A BLAST OF HUNTERS

The reference is to the blast of their horns, but a pun was probably intended.

A STALK OF FORESTERS

A BOAST OF SOLDIERS

A DRIFT OF FISHERMEN

A WAYWARDNESS OF HERDSMEN

The term in The Book of St. Albans *is a Waywardnes of haywardes. That prompted Hodgkin to speculate that* "waywardness *is probably only used because 'wayward' rhymes with 'hayward,' " which fortifies the view that there was a literary motive in the creation of these terms, but leaves open the question of the term's meaning. Perhaps this will help: haywards came in two distinct flavors, the herdsman pictured above; and the hayward who, as estate manager for the lord of the manor, paid, tithed and disciplined the villagers, by whom he was cordially loathed. The OED's definition of wayward as "intractable and wrong-headed" would seem to support the latter interpretation of hayward, Webster's definition, "following one's own capricious inclinations," might support the former. The matter has remained unsettled for 505 years; the reader of this book is impaneled on the final jury.*

A RAGE OF MAIDENS

AN INCREDULITY OF CUCKOLDS

Under rag of colts *I indicated that we would reencounter* rage *in a different context. Here it is, meaning not "anger" but "wantonness." In his 1847* Dictionary of Archaic and Provincial Words, *J. O. Halliwell defines to* rage *as "to romp or play wantonly." Chaucer uses it in that sense in* The Miller's Tale *when he recounts that " . . . Nicholas / Fit with this yonge wyf to rage and pleye, / Whil that hir housbond was at Oseneye." All of which is a rather sad commentary on fifteenth-century maidenhood—or the want of it.*

AN INCREDULITY OF CUCKOLDS *also inspired some digging—that led to fascinating provenances. It appears in the list as* an vncredibilitie of Cocoldis, *which doesn't seem to make much sense: cuckolds have good reason to be incredulous, but no one doubts their existence, which* vncredibilitie *would seem to imply. I assumed that somehow, at some time, "incredibility" must have meant "incredulity" as well and so translated it. Then I began a diffident search for some kind of confirmation. I was surprised to find that the OED, under* uncredible, *gave the expected "incredible" as its first definition, but the definitely unexpected "incredulous" as its second. I had been instinctively right—and now I had proof. What was my proof? The mighty, magisterial* Oxford English Dictionary *says so. But even the OED must support its views, and whom does Dr. Murray offer as his authority? Dame Juliana! "Incredulous," says the OED, and points for proof to "1486 Bk. of St. Albans f vj b, An vncredibilitie of Cocoldis." The logic is suspiciously circular, and it's a bit like being offered your own watch as collateral, but I think I'm ready to settle.*

When Proper Terms *came into my hands twenty-two years after the preceding words were written, I found that the trail Hodgkin broke in 1909 matched mine step for step: "The word* incredibility *is used here in a curious sense, namely, as a synonym for* incredulity: *the only thing that, to them, is incredible is that they are* cocoldis.*"*

A RAGE OF THE TEETH
This is the third term from the end of The Compaýnýs of Beeſtýs and fowlýs. Only rascal of boys *and* disworship of Scots *follow it, and clearly, in the fifteenth century, a toothache was so important—and common—that Dame Juliana couldn't leave* a rage of the teethe *out of her seminal list. As Hodgkin observes, "This is the proper term for a 'yonge gentilman' to use . . . Even when suffering great agony he must remember his position and call it 'A Rage of the teethe'!"*

A WORSHIP OF WRITERS

A reference to the reverence shown by writers to their patrons, and not, alas, vice versa. In his Dictionary, *Dr. Johnson defines* patron *as "commonly a wretch who supports with insolence, and is paid with flattery."*

V

*The
Game of Venery
First Move*

So you see, by 1486 the game of venery was in full swing. There are examples of it in most of the early manuscripts. As noted earlier, the first *Harley Manuscript* gives GAGGLE OF GOSSIPS, and the very early book *The Hors, Shepe, & the Ghoos* contributes A PITY OF PRISONERS and A HASTINESS OF COOKS. The importance of these books in the fifteenth century is indicated by the fact that the last named was one of the first printed by William Caxton in the year that he introduced printing to England. And if we are still inclined to think of the social terms of venery as frivolous, C. E. Hare asserts that A BLAST OF HUNTERS and its fellows "were all probably in use at one time or another." There is of course no canon that gives any of these terms sole possession of the field, but clearly they were once well enough established to take their places with a A FLOCK OF SHEEP and A SCHOOL OF FISH.

But, that the codifiers of these terms knew they were playing a word game is equally clear, from the terms themselves—and the history of the game in the centuries since Caxton. It has never stopped. The reader of this book may already know the popular philological story that usually takes Oxford as its locale. In it four dons, each representing a different academic discipline and therefore a different viewpoint, are flapping along the High when their path is crossed by a small but conspicuous group of prostitutes. The quickest don mutters, "A jam of tarts." The second, obviously a fellow in Music, ripostes, "No, a flourish of strumpets." From the third, apparently an expert on nineteenth-century English literature, "Not at all . . . an essay of Trollope's." The fourth offers, "An anthology of pros." (I have heard versions that included "a pride of loins," "a peal of Jezebels," "a smelting of ores," and even "a troop of horse," but this begins to flog a dead one.)

Besides, the dons' venereal terms, brilliantly constructed as they are, seem to me to obscure the point of the game of venery by drawing attention to both ends of the phrase; that is, not only to the term, "anthology," but its object, already a synonym, "pros." What we are admiring is verbal dexterity and ingenuity; what emerges is not poetry but a joke, not revelation but a chuckle.

There has, of course, through the long history of the game, always been the temptation to make a joke of it, and sometimes the temptation is irresistible. I began playing the game of venery long before I knew that Dame Juliana (or anyone else) had. For a few euphoric days I thought I had invented it. And I have often been tempted by the punning possibilities of the game, as you will see when you encounter A KEROUAC OF DEADBEATS in the Low Life section, but I have declared the illustrious dons' puns *WHORES DE COMBAT*, and struck them from the list that follows.

Having taken this high-handed attitude toward what a term of venery is *not*, I suppose it is incumbent on me to try to explain as precisely as I can what I think it *is*. First of all, obviously, I think it is poetry. Robert Frost wrote, "There are many other things I have found myself saying about poetry, but the chiefest of these is that it is metaphor, saying one thing and meaning another, saying one thing in *terms* of another." (Italics mine.)

Certainly, by this definition the venereal terms are the essence of poetry, the "chiefest" thing, for they are unalloyed metaphor. Specifically, most of them are synechdochic in form, letting a quintessential part (PRIDE, LEAP, GAGGLE, SKULK) stand for the whole, giving us large illuminations in small flashes.

My principal objection to the dons' terms is that they do not say "one thing in terms of another"; they say *two* things, both "essay" and "Trollope's"; and, lost in admiration for the double double entendre (quadruple entendre?), we lose poetry, and illumination too. We have witnessed some verbal sleight-of-hand; but "anthology" and "jam" tell us nothing about whores, and that is, or *should* be, the purpose of the game. At least it is in the best examples I can think of, *e.g.*, A PARLIAMENT OF OWLS—"parliament" tells us something, it gives us a valuable quiddity of owls.

My position on this is, of course, much too dogmatic. A joke may illuminate, and you will find in the list that follows a number of them that I couldn't resist. The only reason I have emphasized this point is that one of the basic rules of the game of venery, is that it is the *term* that matters. In AN EXALTATION OF LARKS, "exaltation" is the operative word. If "larks" had been turned into a synonym that made a *jeu de mots* of the whole phrase, more would have been lost than gained.

In some cases, as perhaps in "a flourish of strumpets," we seem to have both joke and revelation, but, for me, "an anthology of pros" stands somewhere outside the venereal game, the goal of which is to tell us something quintessentially true about the term's object—something we failed to notice or took for granted until that moment. The term of venery is a spotlight that *illuminates* something for us, letting us see it with fresh insight, or as if for the first time.

If you join in the game of venery—and by now it must be apparent that this book is an invitation to—you will probably find that your first attempts are almost all alliterative (like GAGGLE OF GEESE). My advice, for what it is worth, is to fight that impulse. If the proper, poetic, illuminating term happens to be alliterative with the group it is describing, well and good; but if it is not, nothing is lost, and there may be a clearer focus on the main thing: the term, with its gingery secret. In the game of venery, as in the arts, simplicity is the goal and distillation is the way. "Omission," Lytton Strachey wrote in in 1912, "is the beginning of all art," and G. K. Chesterton offered this blunt advice to writers too fond of their tropes to edit them out: "Murder your darlings."

Tautologies should be avoided, since they say the same thing twice, as in "a thought of thinkers." The term must *add* something to the equation.

My final and most emphatic counsel is to take my counsel with a grain of salt. "Any fool can make a rule," Thoreau said in 1860, "and every fool will mind it."

In the five hundred year history of the game of venery there have been a great many players. Toward the end of his scholarly *Language of Field Sports*. C. E. Hare cannot resist a list of contemporary terms that includes AN OBSTINACY OF BUFFALOES, A BASK OF CROCODILES, A TOWER OF GIRAFFES, A POMP OF PEKINGESE, A DEBAUCHERY OF BACHELORS, AN ERUDITION OF EDITORS, AN UNEMPLOYMENT OF GRADUATES, A WOBBLE OF BICYCLES, and A DAWDLING OF WAITERS. Even the staid, scholarly Hodgkin ends his book with a "Solatium" [a consolation, usually a sum of money], taken from *The Visions of Dom Francisco de Quevedo Villegas*, which Hodgkin explains is "here inserted in order to compensate in some slight measure for the destruction of [some of] the 'alleged company terms': A Brace of Devils; A Gang of *Poets*, *Fiddlers*, *Lovers* and *Fencers*; A Knot of Astrologers; A Parcel of Mathematicians; and a Troop of *Women* upon *the High-way to Hell*." Well, Hodgkin had other virtues.

The list that follows consists of the terms of venery that I have coined or encountered since I began unearthing these shards of poetry and truth. I hasten to acknowledge that some of the terms are not mine. A PHALANX OF FLASHERS is Kurt Vonnegut's, A MEWS OF CATHOUSES Neil Simon's, AN OM OF BUDDHISTS George Plimpton's, A METAMORPHOSIS OF OVOIDS Peabody Museum archeologist Ian Graham's; A CHAPTER OF PRINTERS and many keen semantic perceptions are polymath Timothy Dickinson's. Jody Maxmin, a graduate student at Wolfson College, Oxford, drew Martin Robertson, Professor of Classical Archaeology, and Dr. P. R. S. Moorey, Keeper of Near Eastern Antiquities of the Ashmolean Museum, into the game, and sent me a list of dozens of terms, some of which you will find in the following pages; and many of the terms in the Medicine & Health section appeared in medical journals, physicians as a class being far and away the most intrepid players of the game of venery. Freeman Keyte of Nepean, Ontario, out of the goodness of his heart and devotion to the game, went to the considerable trouble of generating and sending me an unsolicited and welcome index of the first edition, which helped enormously in the writing of this one.

A complete roster of the thousands of volunteers who have answered my call to arms would exceed this book's allotment of signatures, so to all who have contributed collectives—collectively—a deep, and deeply grateful, bow.

As you can see from these acknowledgements, each time I have played the game of venery, like Tom Sawyer whitewashing his fence, I have found that spectators didn't stay spectators long. If you should feel the urge, there are more brushes in the bucket.

People, Places & Things

A *BON TON* OF FRENCH WOMEN

A *SAVOIR FAIRE* OF FRENCHMEN
A POUND OF ENGLISHMEN
A PINT OF IRISHMEN
A FIFTH OF SCOTS
A BOOM OF GERMANS
AN ESPRESSO OF ITALIANS
AN EDELWEISS OF AUSTRIANS
A WATCH OF SWISS
A SMORGASBORD OF SWEDES
A GOULASH OF HUNGARIANS
A CC OF SPANIARDS
AN ATTIC OF GREEKS
AN APPARAT OF SOVIETS
versus
A GLASNOST OF RUSSIANS
A SOLIDARITY OF POLES
A VENDETTA OF SICILIANS
A WAVE OF HAWAIIANS
AN OUTBACK OF AUSSIES

A KENDO OF JAPANESE *Pronounced "can do."*

A DILIGENCE OF KOREANS

A CRUSH OF CHINESE
Used, alas, in both senses: of multitude and 1989 official behavior.

A CAST OF INDIANS

AN IMBROGLIO OF ISRAELIS
       LEBANESE
       SYRIANS
       IRAQUIS
        etc., etc., etc.
Good luck and good will may someday render this term obsolete.

A *KOMITEH* OF IRANIANS
The Komiteh *(Committee) is the national disciplinary patrol responsible for enforcing Islamic regulations of social behavior.*

A *TABERNAC* OF FRENCH CANADIANS

A *MARIACHI* OF MEXICANS

A *BOSSA NOVA* OF BRAZILIANS

A *GAÎTÉ* OF PARISIENNES

A BROLLY OF LONDONERS

A MASS OF BOSTONIANS

AN UPYOURS OF NEW YORKERS

A FLOW OF CALIFORNIANS

A SPREAD OF TEXANS

A SPECK OF RHODE ISLANDERS

A GAMBOL OF NEVADANS

A JULEP OF KENTUCKIANS

A BASK OF FLORIDIANS

A MUSH OF ALASKANS

A STORE OF GYPSIES

A VIGILANCE OF ENVIRONMENTALISTS

AN EXPLOSION OF BABY BOOMERS

A SHORTAGE OF MIDGETS

A WHEEL OF ROTARIANS

A MAGNET OF BARGAINS

A CHARGE OF SHOPPERS

AN EMBARRASSMENT OF BEEPERS
E.g. during the first act of a play or any act of seduction.

A SHOCK OF ALARMS
Unlike beepers (q.v.), alarms invariably go off in the middle of the night, except in the event of an actual emergency, when they turn into a silence of alarms.

AN INTRUSION OF ANSWERING MACHINES

A BELLOW OF BOOMBOXES

A BABEL OF CELLULAR PHONES

A DRONE OF AIR CONDITIONERS

A PHUMPHER OF SCHWAS

Here's a pretty how-de-do: another collective of collectives. The Greek language borrowed the schwa *from Hebrew, which represented it by what we would call a colon. Indo-European linguistics adopted the* schwa *from the Greek as a phonetic symbol, in the form of the inverted* e *(see the illustration) we encounter in dictionaries denoting the neutral central vowel in unstressed syllables: the* e *in* quiet, *for example. However, language pundit William Safire insists that all the "ers" and "uhs" we utter are schwas as well, and one challenges Safire at one's linguistic peril. So, Mr. Safire, how about* a phumpher of schwas?

A TRANSPARENCY OF TOUPEES

A RASH OF HEATWAVES

A LATITUDE OF MAPS

A GENERATION OF SPERM BANKS

A PAVEMENT OF GOOD INTENTIONS

A QUICK-CHANGE OF NEW YEARS RESOLUTIONS

AN EXPLOSION OF THEORIES

A RUBBLE OF REPUTATIONS

AN INEVITABILITY OF COMEUPPANCES

A METAMORPHOSIS OF OVOIDS
Term for hatching eggs in 1st-century Rome.

AN EXULTATION OF FIREWORKS

Since the publication of the first edition of this book, I have been asked occasionally: why exaltation *and not* exultation *of larks? The answer is that both* exult *and* exalt *existed when the terms were codified, and the codifiers, without exception, chose* exaltation, *which can have either the sense of "praising" (the sky, the moment, life), or of "an exalted state," which Webster describes as "an intensified sense of well-being." That hasn't stilled the voices of those partial to "the joyful leaping up" of* exultation, *so, to mollify that faction, this ultimate edition offers* an exultation of fireworks.

Professions

A CHISEL OF REPAIRMEN

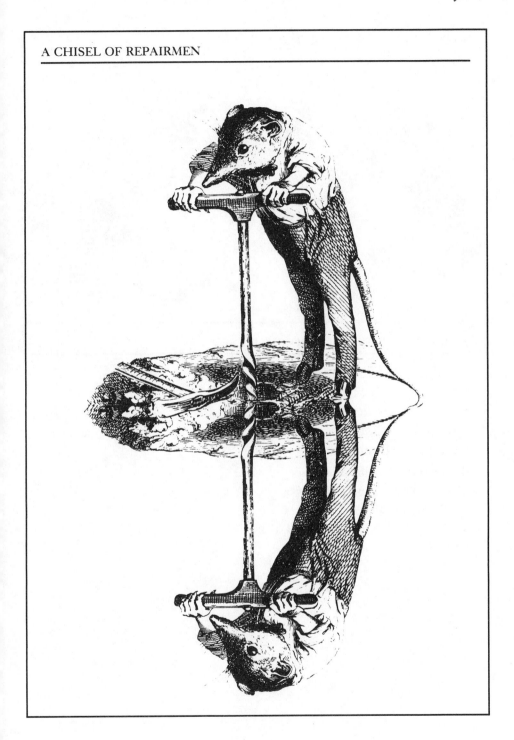

A RENDERING OF ARCHITECTS

A RENDING OF CONTRACTORS

A PILING OF CONSTRUCTION WORKERS

AN OHM OF ELECTRICIANS

A FLUSH OF PLUMBERS

A CLAMBER OF ROOFERS

A DRIP OF HOUSEPAINTERS

A CRASH OF GLAZIERS

A PANEL OF CARPENTERS

A QUANTUM OF MECHANICS

AN INERTIA OF JANITORS

A SNOOZE OF NIGHTWATCHMEN

A SESAME OF LOCKSMITHS

A SAMPLE OF SALESMEN

AN AROMA OF BAKERS

A SUITE OF CONFECTIONERS

A NOSEGAY OF FLORISTS

A RING OF JEWELERS

A SHUTTLE OF WEAVERS

A COTE OF TAILORS
See the note on cete of badgers

A RAP OF FURRIERS

AN ALIEN-NATION OF MIGRANT WORKERS

A BABBLE OF BARBERS

A FILE OF MANICURISTS

A HAGGLE OF VENDORS

A LOT OF REALTORS
AN AMBUSH OF USED-CAR DEALERS
A TRUCULENCE OF MOVING MEN
A SAUNTER OF COWBOYS
A PLAIN OF FARMERS
A COALITION OF MINERS

A TRINE OF ASTROLOGERS

A LINE OF PALMISTS

AN AMPHIBOLY OF PSYCHICS

Shakespeare uses amphiboly, the logical fallacy of ambiguity, when the spirit prophesies to Henry VI that "The Duke yet lives that Henry shall depose," which Henry takes to mean he is going to depose a Duke, when it can as easily mean a Duke is going to depose Henry. Amphiboly, in a word, is how some of the people on this page stay in business.

A GUESS OF FUTURISTS

A DOODLE OF GRAPHOLOGISTS

AN OSTENTATION OF PORTENTS AND PRODIGIES

We have seen ostentation *in another sense.* Topsell's Foure-footed Beastes *speaks of "predictions or ostentations of things to come," and the OED gives as its first definition of* ostentation, *"Presage; a portent, prodigy."*

Home & Family

A PERSISTENCE OF PARENTS
AN INGRATITUDE OF CHILDREN
A CONSTERNATION OF MOTHERS
A DISTRACTION OF FATHERS
A SUFFOCATION OF AUNTS
A BLUSTER OF UNCLES

A MUTTER OF MOTHERS-IN-LAW

A CLUTCH OF FAMILIES
No less an authority for this term than the Oxford English Dictionary; see clutch of eggs.

A NO-NO OF NANNIES

In clement weather A PERAMBULATION OF NANNIES.

A GIGGLE OF GIRLS

A GOGGLE OF BOYS

AN ACNE OF ADOLESCENTS

A TUMESCENCE OF PUBESCENTS

A CONSERVATORY OF ORPHANS
Ever wondered what a conservatory conserves? In the seventeenth century orphans were consigned to conservatories *where, traditionally, they were taught music; hence the* conservatory of music.

A STOOP OF ELDERS

A PROWL OF WIDOWS

A CAPER OF KIDS

Another quadruple entendre that merits attention at both ends of the phrase. In slang that has become proper English, children are often called kids *because their antics resemble those of a young goat, which was called in Middle English* kide, *a word with much earlier antecedents in the Norse and Teutonic languages. While grown-up goats acquired their stolid English-language name from the Middle English* goot *and the Anglo-Saxon* gat, *in the Latin linguistic line, goat is* capra, *which muscled its way into English alongside* goat *in such words as* Capricorn *(goat-horned):* Capra, *the name of the genus to which goats belong;* caprice; capricious; capricioso, *the musical direction for a free and fanciful style;* capriole, *which the OED gives as a variant root for* caper, *and defines as "a frolicsome leap, like that of a playful kid"; and finally in the lively word* caper—*which also identifies a Mediterranean shrub cultivated for its aromatic buds. Here the ring closes, for it is from those buds, the goat's favorite delicacy, that the goat gets its Latin name, as does the island of Capri, which swarmed, when it was the resort of Rome's emperors, with goats—and capers, of the botanic, gymnastic and erotic varieties. Come to think of it,* a caper of kids *may be this book's first sextuple entendre.*

A TANTRUM OF DECORATORS

A WOBBLE OF ANTIQUES

A HAMMER OF AUCTIONEERS

A NOD OF BIDDERS

AN OBSOLESCENCE OF APPLIANCES

A RANGE OF OVENS

A *MAL DE MER* OF WATERBEDS

A CONGESTION OF CLOSETS

A JANGLE OF HANGERS

A TITILLATION OF LINGERIE

A STAIN OF NECKTIES

A SQUEAK OF SNEAKERS

A BILLBOARD OF T-SHIRTS

A SHUDDER OF WASHING MACHINES

A LOAD OF DIAPERS

A DESCENT OF RELATIVES

A BREACH OF PREMISES
Law-enforcement terminology for a case of breaking and entering by a former husband, wife, or lover.

A NERVE OF NEIGHBORS

AN EXPECTATION OF HEIRS

A COMPLAINT OF TENANTS

A LACHES OF LANDLORDS

A YECH! OF COCKROACHES

A SLEW OF EXTERMINATORS

A *DÉJÀ GOUT* OF LEFTOVERS

The anglicized spelling, goo, *is equally acceptable—and unpalatable.*

A BROMIDE OF GREETING CARDS

A SWAMP OF JUNK MAIL

A QUICKSAND OF CREDIT CARDS

A LOSS OF UMBRELLAS

A SPRINKLING OF GARDENERS

A RASP OF LAWNMOWERS

Daily Life

A STRANGLE OF CITY DWELLERS

A LURCH OF BUSES

A WHIPLASH OF POTHOLES

A PUREE OF STRAPHANGERS

A CHARGE OF TAXIS
In Tokyo, an overcharge of taxis

A DROVE OF CABDRIVERS

A CALCUTTA OF PANHANDLERS

A HAIL OF DOORMEN

A DELAY OF DELIVERYMEN

A CHIME OF ICE CREAM CARTS

A PLUCK OF FIREFIGHTERS

A GRIND OF SANITATION MEN

A ROUND OF MAILMEN

A WAIL OF SIRENS

A HUDDLE OF HOMELESS

A COLD SHOULDER OF PASSERSBY
A YO! OF STREET KIDS
A YO YO OF STREET GANGS
AN EYESORE OF GRAFFITI
A ROT OF GARBAGE
A FOREST OF ANTENNAS
A BELCH OF SMOKESTACKS
A DASH OF COMMUTERS
A TRANSPLANT OF SUBURBANITES
A SPRAWL OF MALLS
A SAMBA OF SHOPPING CARTS
A BOOTY OF BOUTIQUES

High Life

AN ENNUI OF THE *HAUTE BOURGEOSIE*

A SNEER OF BUTLERS

A DELIRIUM OF DEBUTANTES

A FROST OF DOWAGERS

In his poem Goodnight to the Season, *Winthrop Mackworth Praed remarks on "The ice of her Ladyship's manners,/The ice of his Lordship's Champagne."*

AN UPPITY OF SNOBS

A SNIFF OF HEADWAITERS

AN INDIFFERENCE OF WAITERS

A SPILL OF BUSBOYS

A SOUPÇON OF CHEFS
Pronounced "Soup's on!" in rural areas.

A FUMBLE OF CHECKGRABBERS

A POUF OF HAIRDRESSERS

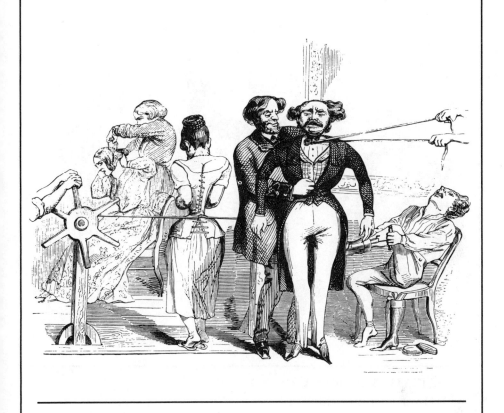

A MARTYRDOM OF FASHION-SLAVES

AN ENSEMBLE OF COUTURIERS

A BOULEVARD OF BON VIVANTS
Which intersects the Boulevard of Broken Dreams.

A DELICATESSE OF GOURMETS

A DELICATESSEN OF GOURMANDS

A CANAPÉ OF CATERERS

A SCLEROSIS OF FAST FOODS

A BUZZ OF BARFLIES

A BLARNEY OF BARTENDERS
This is simply a contemporary rendition of St. Alban's A Glosyng of Tauerneris, q.v. *in the note to* A CAJOLERY OF TAVERNERS, *Part IV.*

A STREAK OF GAMBLERS

A TRIP OF HIPPIES
Archaic. How time flies.

A CONSUMPTION OF YUPPIES *See preceding note.*

A RELISH OF CONNOISSEURS

A BOUQUET OF WINETASTERS

The following seven terms are genuine collectives, coined by Champagne merchants in the late nineteenth century to indicate the equivalent number of wine bottles in each of these outsize bottles.

A MAGNUM *2 bottles.*

A JEROBOAM *(king of the newly-formed northern kingdom of Israel) 4 bottles, serving 24 people, traditionally used for ship christenings.*

A REHOBOAM *(son of Solomon, the first king to reign over Judah) 6 bottles, serving 36.*

A METHUSELAH *(the only eponym who was not a king, but lived to the age of 969) 8 bottles, serving 48, with no guarantee of longevity.*

A SALMANAZAR *(Syrian king who ruled over the Judean kingdom) 12 bottles (a case), serving 72.*

A BALTHAZAR *(one of the Magi) 16 bottles, serving 96.*

A NEBUCHADNEZZAR *(king of Babylon) 20 bottles, serving 120, or W.C. Fields, Jackie Gleason and Henry VIII at an intimate Valhallan dinner.*

A STEIN OF BEER
From the German steingut, *stoneware. The Germans know beer.*

UN *SÉRIEUX DE BIÈRE*
So do the French. Since Champagne isn't the only consommation, *the French decreed: if you want your beer in that really big goblet behind the bar of the* brasserie, *demandez un sérieux.*

A LADDER OF SOCIAL CLIMBERS

Low Life

A PHALANX OF FLASHERS

A SLAVER OF GLUTTONS

A ROOD OF BOORS

A HEEP OF SYCOPHANTS
Our term is Dickensian; the German language, with typical scientific precision, further defines the breed, giving us the useful term Radfahrer *for the person we've all encountered who kisses the behinds above, and kicks those below.*

A HORDE OF MISERS

AN OFFAL OF POLLUTERS

A KLAVERN OF KLANSMEN

A GALLERY OF ROGUES

A CHATTER OF FINKS
See A CHARM OF FINCHES.

A DISH OF GOSSIPS

A BELLYFUL OF BORES

A CURSE OF CREDITORS

A KEROUAC OF DEADBEATS

A STALL OF PROCRASTINATORS

A LOAD OF DRUNKS

A BAG OF JUNKIES
In England: A stone of junkies.

A PESTILENCE OF CRACK

A VIAL (*variant:* VILE) OF DEALERS

A COFFLE OF SLAVES
Sadly, a collective term once in common use for a line of slaves, chained together; from the Arabic qafila *(caravan).*

A BOOTH OF ASSASSINS

A MASK OF EXECUTIONERS

Romance & Raunch

A TRANCE OF LOVERS

A GARLAND OF POEMS
If Dame Juliana was "England's earliest poetess," as Blades claimed, the no-blewoman Sulpicia was one of Rome's when she wrote a volume of love lyrics, Sulpicia's Garland, *in the first century B. C.*

A THRILL OF BRIDES

A THRALL OF BRIDEGROOMS

A SLOUCH OF MODELS

A RICTUS OF BEAUTY QUEENS

A SCORE OF BACHELORS

A FREEZE (*archaic:* FRIEZE) OF VIRGINS

A HANGOUT OF NUDISTS

A SPREAD OF CENTERFOLDS
See SPREAD OF PAGES *in Arts and Letters*.

A MEWS OF CATHOUSES

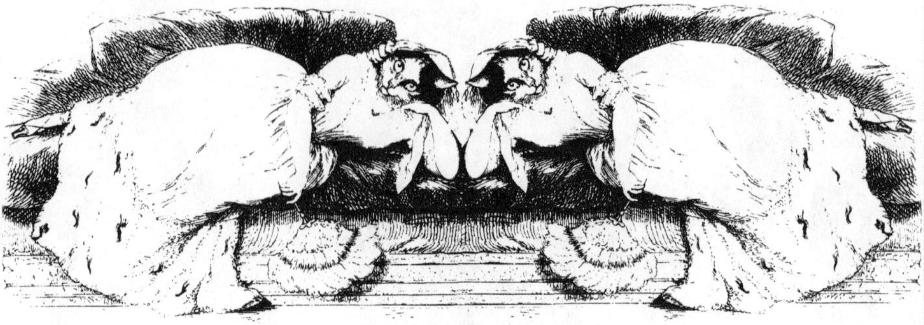

A EUPHEMISM OF ESCORT SERVICES

A PANDER OF PORNOGRAPHERS

A MOUNT OF PORN STARS

A RACK OF SADOMASOCHISTS

A KEYHOLE OF VOYEURS

A HOTBED OF SWINGERS

A CONCATENATION OF ORGIASTS

A LUBRICITY OF NYMPHOMANIACS

A RUT OF SATYRS

A LECH OF DIRTY OLD MEN

A FALSETTO OF TRANSVESTITES

Medicine & Health

A FAMILY OF GENERAL PRACTITIONERS

A PALPATION OF INTERNISTS
A FIBRILLATION OF CARDIOLOGISTS
A HANDFUL OF GYNECOLOGISTS
A STIRRUP OF OBSTETRICIANS

A STAPH OF DIAGNOSTICIANS

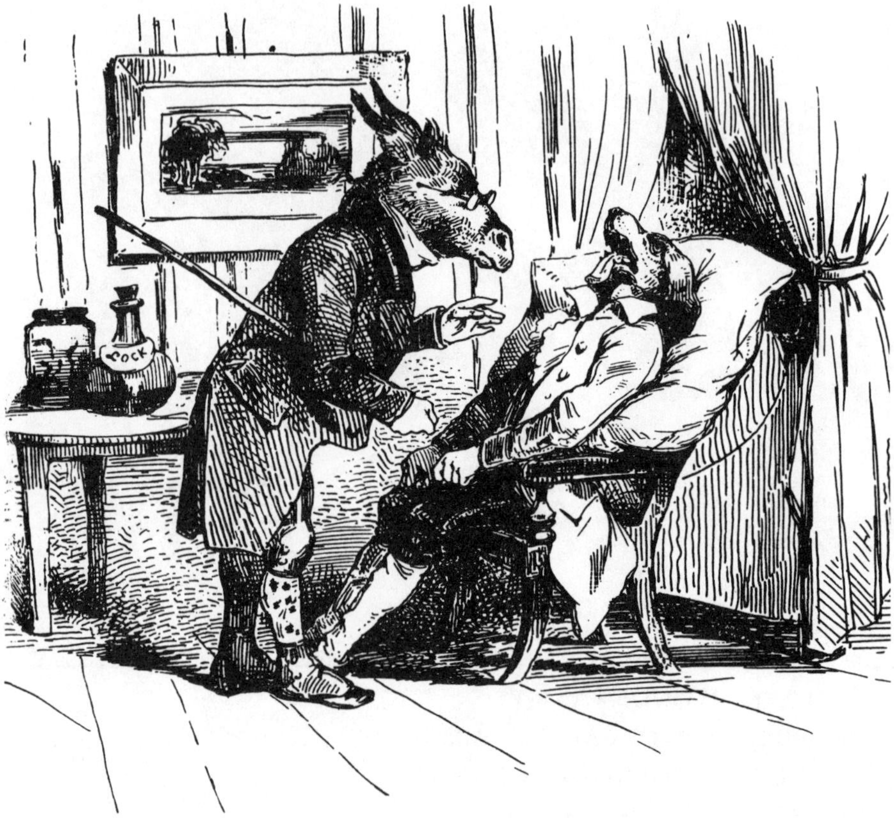

A RASH OF DERMATOLOGISTS
A VOID OF UROLOGISTS
A PILE OF PROCTOLOGISTS
A MOVEMENT OF GASTROENTEROLOGISTS
A LUMP OF ONCOLOGISTS

A HIVE OF ALLERGISTS

A SHOT OF PEDIATRICIANS

A VOCATION OF LARYNGOLOGISTS

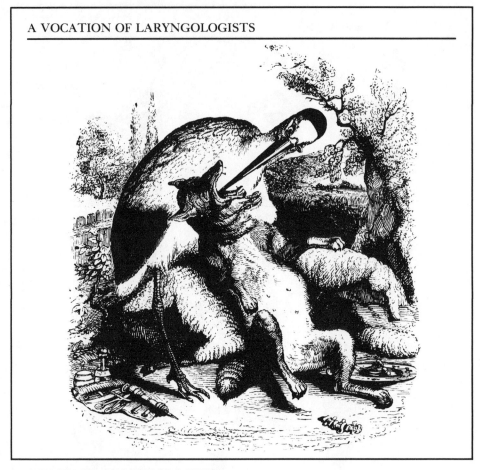

A PASSAGE OF RHINOLOGISTS

A HERD OF OTOLOGISTS

A RETINUE OF OPHTHALMOLOGISTS

A GOUT OF RHEUMATOLOGISTS

A VEIN OF HEMATOLOGISTS

A CAST OF ORTHOPEDISTS

A JOINT OF OSTEOPATHS

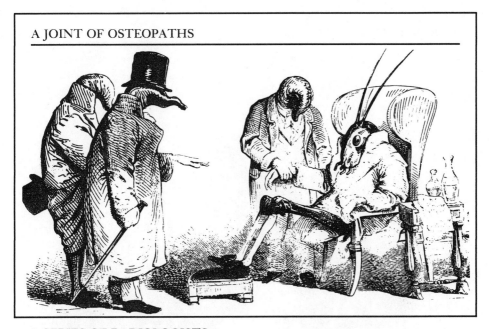

A SERIES OF RADIOLOGISTS
AN ARCH OF PODIATRISTS
A COLONY OF BACTERIOLOGISTS
A PLAGUE OF EPIDEMIOLOGISTS
A HELIX OF GENETICISTS
A HOST OF PARASITOLOGISTS
A BATCH OF VIROLOGISTS

A RESECT OF SURGEONS

A BURR OF NEUROSURGEONS

A BAG OF ANESTHESIOLOGISTS

A DEARTH OF NURSES

A SLEEPWALK OF RESIDENTS

A PAN OF ORDERLIES

A TRAY OF DIETICIANS

A PESTLE OF PHARMACISTS

A PHARMACOPOEIA OF NOSTRUMS

A KILLING OF MEDICAL INSURERS

A TERMINUS OF THANATOLOGISTS

AN UNCTION OF UNDERTAKERS

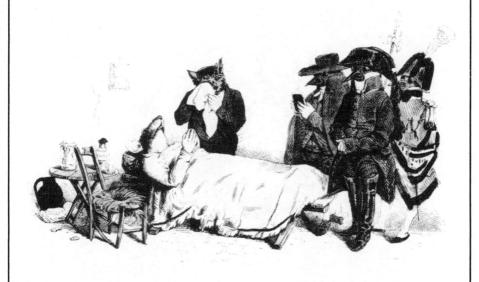

A larger group: AN EXTREME UNCTION OF UNDERTAKERS

A GROSS OF PATHOLOGISTS

A CORPS OF ANATOMISTS

A STING OF ACUPUNCTURISTS

A CRACK OF CHIROPRACTORS

A POWWOW OF VETERINARIANS

AN EMBARRASSMENT OF TWITCHES

A COMPLEX OF PSYCHOANALYSTS

A PANIC OF PARANOIDS

A SPLIT OF SCHIZOIDS

A KVETCH OF HYPOCHONDRIACS

A CONGRESS OF SEXOLOGISTS

A WINCE OF DENTISTS

A BRACE OF ORTHODONTISTS
A PLAQUE OF PERIODONTISTS
A CANAL OF ENDODONTISTS

A POT OF DIETERS

A CONFLAB OF WEIGHTWATCHERS

A BURN OF FITNESS VIDEOTAPES

A JUNGLE OF HEALTH CLUBS

A PUMMEL OF MASSEURS

A CARNAGE OF CIGARETTES
Formerly carton

A PACK OF SMOKERS

A HACK OF HEAVY SMOKERS

A HAZE OF CIGAR SMOKERS

Academe

A FAILING OF STUDENTS

A DILATION OF PUPILS *in Dr. Leary's era*

A LACK OF PRINCIPALS

A PLENITUDE OF FRESHMEN

A PLATITUDE OF SOPHOMORES

A GRATITUDE OF JUNIORS

AN ATTITUDE OF SENIORS

A FORTITUDE OF GRADUATE STUDENTS

A *VALE* OF GRADUATES

A DOGGEDNESS OF DOCTORAL CANDIDATES

AN *ANGST* OF DISSERTATIONS

A KEY OF PHI BETA KAPPAS

AN EX CATHEDRA OF PROFESSORS EMERITI

A CLAMBER OF ASSISTANT PROFESSORS
A TENURE OF ASSOCIATE PROFESSORS
AN ENTROPY OF FULL PROFESSORS

A BORED OF TRUSTEES

A PURSESTRING OF ALUMNI

AN OVERSIGHT OF DEANS

A DROWSE OF UNDERACHIEVERS

A LEAP OF OVERACHIEVERS

A PALLOR OF NIGHT STUDENTS

AN OXYMORON OF ATHLETIC SCHOLARSHIPS

A CUDDLE OF HOMECOMING QUEENS

A WRANGLE OF PHILOSOPHERS

A VICIOUS CIRCLE OF FALLACIES

A FORM OF PLATONISTS

A CATEGORY OF ARISTOTELIANS

A PORCH OF STOICS

A CULTURE OF EPICUREANS

A WALK OF PERIPATETICS

AN INTROSPECTION OF SOLIPSISTS

A NULLITY OF NIHILISTS

A PREMISE OF LOGICIANS

A TRANSCENDANCE OF METAPHYSICIANS

A BARK OF CYNICS

In the fourth century B.C., the Cynics were nicknamed "dogs" because they took the name of their philosophical school from the Cynosarges *gymnasium, the first two syllables of which can be read to mean* doglike. *Diogenes, the archetypal Cynic, who argued the case for the Cynics' anarchistic "natural" life by searching for an honest man with a lantern in broad daylight, was buried in a tomb crowned proudly and defiantly by a marble dog.*

A SUMMA OF THOMISTS

A TABULA RASA OF EMPIRICISTS

AN ESSENCE OF EXISTENTIALISTS

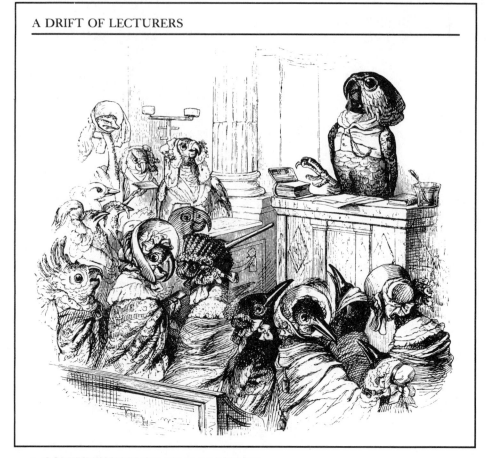

A DRIFT OF LECTURERS

A CONJUNCTION OF GRAMMARIANS

A GLOSS OF PHILOLOGISTS

A LAPSUS OF LINGUISTS

A LOGORRHEA OF LEXICOGRAPHERS

A CONSPIRACY OF CRYPTOLOGISTS

A SHELF OF CLASSICISTS

A PRAISE OF CLASSICS

Apparently confident that his bucolic tales would never qualify for this dubious honor, Mark Twain defined a "classic" as "a book which people praise and don't read." In the same vein, Voltaire remarked that Dante's reputation grows continuously because hardly anyone reads him.

A SHUSH OF LIBRARIANS

A TROVE OF LIBRARIES

A BROOD OF RESEARCHERS

A DISCORD OF EXPERTS

Science & Technology

A GALAXY OF ASTRONOMERS

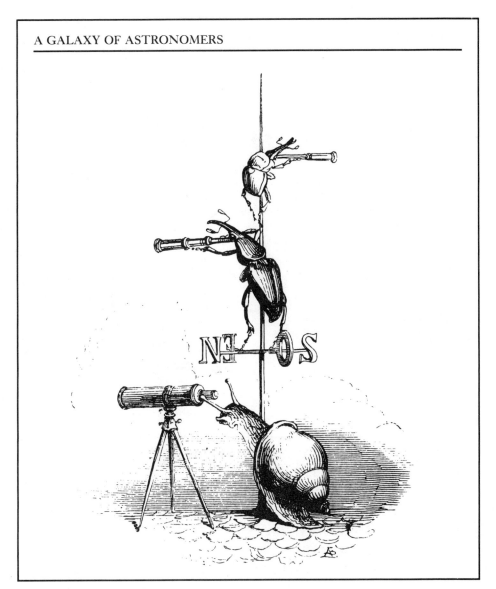

A BELT OF ASTEROIDS

A TRAJECTORY OF ASTRONAUTS

AN APOGEE OF SATELLITES

A QUINCUNX OF OBJECTS
A proper term for any group of five objects placed in a square, with four of the objects at the square's corners and one at its center.

A SHELL OF ELECTRONS

A SHOWER OF METEOROLOGISTS

AN ERUPTION OF VULCANOLOGISTS

A NUCLEUS OF PHYSICISTS

A COLLOID OF CHEMISTS

A FAMILY OF BIOLOGISTS

A TRIBE OF ANTHROPOLOGISTS

A STRATUM OF GEOLOGISTS

AN ENTRENCHMENT OF ARCHEOLOGISTS

A PYRAMID OF EGYPTOLOGISTS

A FILLET OF PALEONTOLOGISTS

A FORMICATION OF ENTOMOLOGISTS

A WEB OF ARACHNOLOGISTS

A NUCLEAR FAMILY OF SOCIOLOGISTS

AN EXTENDED FAMILY OF SOCIOLOGISTS
In a larger group.

A PULLULATION OF MICROBIOLOGISTS

A NUMBER OF STATISTICIANS

A SET OF MATHEMATICIANS

A GOOGOL OF PARTICLES

When the American mathematician Edward Kasner wondered aloud what to call the figure 1 followed by 100 zeroes, his nine-year-old nephew proposed googol, *and googol it is, in frequent and proper use for any ten things raised to the power of a hundred—or any unthinkably large quantity.*

A BYTE OF COMPUTER OPERATORS

A MEGABYTE OF COMPUTER PROGRAMMERS

A WYSIWYG OF COMPUTER PROGRAMS

Computerese for What You See (on the screen) Is What You Get (on the printed page).

A DISCOURSE OF FAX MACHINES

AN ARGOS OF VCR'S

A SYZYGY OF STARS

A nearly straight-line configuration of three heavenly bodies, e.g. the sun, moon and earth during an eclipse, or Miss America, Miss Universe and Madonna at a checkout counter.

A BOO! OF TERATOLOGISTS
Teratology is the biological study of monsters.

A TREE OF GENEALOGISTS
In a smaller group: a branch.

Sports

FOOTBALL

A HUDDLE OF PLAYERS

A CUSS OF COACHES

A RUN OF BACKS

A TARGET OF WIDE RECEIVERS

A POCKET OF QUARTERBACKS

A SACK OF LINEBACKERS

AN INTERFERENCE OF CORNERBACKS

A PIT OF LINEMEN

A WEDGE OF BLOCKERS

A FRENZY OF CHEERLEADERS

BASEBALL

A CROUCH OF CATCHERS

A MOUND OF PITCHERS
Collectively, the pitcher and catcher are a battery.

A DECK OF BATTERS

A SPIT OF BENCHWARMERS

A MYOPIA OF UMPIRES

A WAVE OF BASEBALL FANS

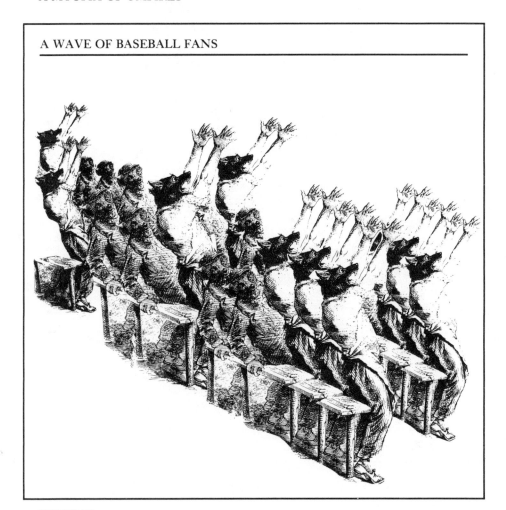

HOCKEY

A FACEOFF OF CENTERS

A SCORE OF FORWARDS

A SLASH OF DEFENSEMEN

A SPRAWL OF GOALIES

A HOWL OF HOCKEY FANS

BASKETBALL
A DRIBBLE OF GUARDS
A LIFTOFF OF FORWARDS
A BLOCK OF CENTERS
AN OOPS OF TURNOVERS
A CONNIPTION OF COACHES
A BLINDNESS OF REFEREES

AN OUTRAGE OF BASKETBALL FANS

TRACK AND FIELD
A SPLIT OF HURDLERS
A SPLAT OF HIGH-JUMPERS
A GLIDE OF LONG-JUMPERS
A SLINGSHOT OF POLE-VAULTERS
AN EXPLOSION OF SPRINTERS
A GRIND OF MARATHONERS
A GRUNT OF SHOT-PUTTERS
A SQUAT OF WEIGHT-LIFTERS

A RING OF BOXERS

A BUZZ OF FLYWEIGHTS
A LIGHTNING OF LIGHTWEIGHTS
A THUNDER OF HEAVYWEIGHTS
A BREAKDANCE OF REFEREES
A SWARM OF SECONDS
A CLUTCH OF MANAGERS
A QUARREL OF COMMISSIONERS

A SLAM OF WRESTLERS
A GRAND SLAM OF TAG TEAM WRESTLERS
A MOUNTAIN OF SUMO WRESTLERS
A CHOP OF MARTIAL ARTISTS

A TUMBLE OF GYMNASTS

A POSE OF BODY BUILDERS

A PERCH OF JOCKEYS

A PARLAY OF HORSEPLAYERS

A PITCH OF SOCCER PLAYERS

A SCRUM OF RUGBY PLAYERS

A ROQUET OF CROQUET PLAYERS

A MASSE OF POOL PLAYERS

A VOLLEY OF TENNIS PLAYERS

A BATTLE OF BADMINTON PLAYERS

A SMASH OF PING-PONG PLAYERS

A DRAFT OF RACING DRIVERS

A RAFT OF SWIMMERS

A TUBE OF SURFERS

A PRANCE OF EQUESTRIANS

A PAVANE OF MATADORS

A LEAP OF BANDERILLEROS

AN AXEL OF FIGURE SKATERS

A *SCHUSS* OF SKIERS

A GRAPPLE OF ROCK-CLIMBERS

AN UPRISING OF MOUNTAINEERS

A ROUT OF SNOWMOBILES

A ROD OF FISHERMEN

A ROW OF OARSMEN

A LIE OF GOLFERS

A SKITTER OF GOLF CARTS

A BOWL OF KEGLERS
or vice versa

A WHEEZE OF JOGGERS

Games & Recreation

A MELD OF GIN PLAYERS

A MEDDLE OF KIBITZERS

A STUD OF POKER PLAYERS

A CONTRACT OF BRIDGE HANDS

A GAMBIT OF CHESS MASTERS

A PONDER OF CHECKER PLAYERS

A CATCHWORD OF CROSSWORD PUZZLERS

A LOGOMANIA OF SCRABBLERS

A PAC OF VIDEO GAMESTERS

A STAMPEDE OF PHILATELISTS

A HOARD OF NUMISMATISTS

A PATCH OF QUILTERS

A GLAZE OF TOURISTS

A NECKLACE OF CAMERAS

A TRUDGE OF TOURS

A WELTSCHMERZ OF GUIDES

A MARCH OF MUSEUMS
At the Louvre, Prado, Hermitage and Metropolitan: A LONG MARCH

A RESERVATION OF RESTAURANTS
For the outcome of the reservation, *see* SNIFF OF HEADWAITERS.

AN EVANESCENCE OF TRAVELERS' CHEQUES

A OUI OUI OF PISSOIRS

A PEEL OF SUNBATHERS

A BROILER OF BEACHES

A BLANKET OF PICNICS

A BLAZE OF BARBECUES

A TUG OF KITES

A FLUTTER OF ULTRALIGHTS

A RIPCORD OF SKYDIVERS

Music

A SCHREI OF HELDENTENOREN

A RUMBLE OF BASSES

A QUAVER OF COLORATURAS

A BACKSEAT OF ACCOMPANISTS

A SPATE OF BARITONES

A SPITE OF PRIMA DONNAS

A MOUTHING OF PROMPTERS

A SHRIEK OF CLAQUES

A CORD OF WOODWINDS

A *BRIO* OF CONDUCTORS

A POUND OF PIANISTS

AN OOMPAH OF TUBA PLAYERS

A REST OF TRIANGLE PLAYERS

A PROCESSIONAL OF ORGANISTS

A SKIRL OF BAGPIPERS

A FRET OF GUITARISTS

A FLOURISH OF HERALDS

A RUFFLE OF DRUMMERS

A SECOND-FIDDLE OF VIOLISTS

AN EMBOUCHURE OF BRASS PLAYERS

A METER OF PERCUSSIONISTS

A PARENTHESIS OF CELLISTS

A FLUTTER OF FLUTISTS

A FLATULENCE OF BASSOONISTS

A GLISSANDO OF CLARINETISTS

A BACKACHE OF DOUBLE BASSISTS

A PLAINT OF OBOISTS

A STRING OF VIOLINISTS

A SWEET OF WALTZES

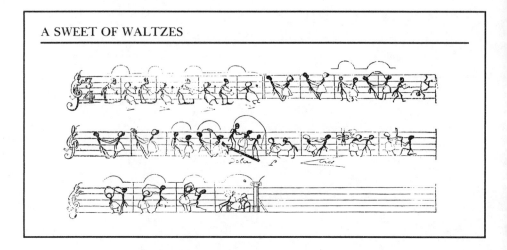

A HUM OF HYMNS

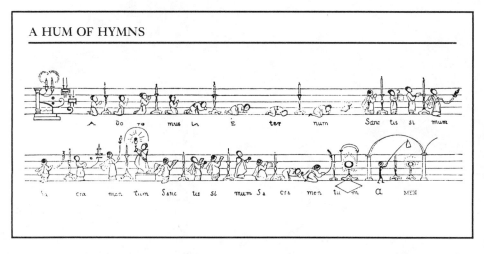

A GRANDIOSITY OF OPERAS

Voltaire on opera libretti: "What is too stupid to be spoken is sung."

A FLOTILLA OF BARCAROLES

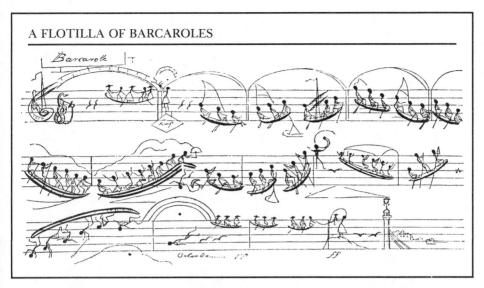

In Italian, a barca *is a boat (whence* bark *in English), a* barcaruolo *is a gondolier, and a* barcarole *is the distinctive 6/8 song that accompanies his stroke.* A flotilla of barcaroles, *and the terms for* waltzes, blues, rondos, hymns *and* opera *are included as much for Grandville's ingenious pictorialization of sound as for the terms. As noted earlier, most of the illustrations in this book are reproductions or adaptations of Grandville's work, and these two pages are an homage to his boundless imagination.*

A RHAPSODY OF BLUES

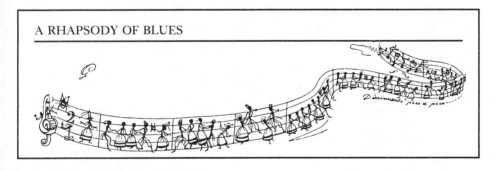

A CAROUSEL OF RONDOS

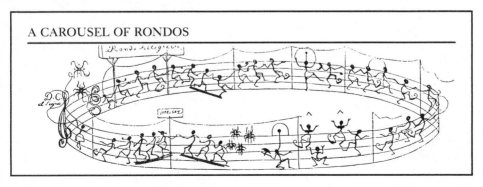

AN UNDULATION OF BALLROOM DANCERS

A GYRATION OF DISCO DANCERS

AN OSCILLATION OF BREAK DANCERS

A CHORUS OF COMPOSERS

A BRIDGE OF LYRICISTS

A STAFF OF ORCHESTRATORS

A RAVEUP OF ROCKERS

A SPASM OF HARD ROCKERS

A PAROXYSM OF PUNK ROCKERS

AN ATTITUDE OF RAPPERS

A GROPE OF GROUPIES

A CLAMOR OF CLUBS

A JUMP-CUT OF MUSIC VIDEOS

A DECIBEL OF DJ'S

A GLOW OF AMPLIFIERS

A FEEDBACK OF SPEAKERS

A TANGLE OF SPOTLIGHTS

Stage

A QUEUE OF ACTORS

AN ENTRANCE OF ACTRESSES

A PREEN OF LEADING LADIES
A PRIDE OF LEADING MEN
AN INNOCENCE OF INGENUES
A TART OF SOUBRETTES
A PANIC OF PRODUCERS
A GILD OF DIRECTORS
A PLOT OF PLAYWRIGHTS

A SET OF DESIGNERS
A BRACE OF STAGEHANDS
A LUMEN OF LIGHTING DIRECTORS
A WHISPER OF STAGE MANAGERS
A MEASURE OF WARDROBE PERSONS
A PIT OF MUSICIANS
AN EAGERNESS OF BOX OFFICES
In a flop

A DEAFNESS OF BOX OFFICES *In a hit*

A SHRIVEL OF CRITICS

A MISDIRECTION OF MAGICIANS
A STRIP OF ECDYSIASTS
or
A TITILLATION OF STRIPPERS
A *BONHOMIE OF* MC'S
A PUNCHLINE OF COMEDIANS
A PRATFALL OF CLOWNS
A DUMBSHOW OF MUMMERS

A FLOAT OF DANCERS (*Female*)

A FLIGHT OF DANCERS (*Male*)

AN ASSEMBLEÉ OF CHOREOGRAPHERS
A CONTRACTION OF MODERN DANCERS
A CONVULSION OF BELLY DANCERS

Screen

A FADE IN (AND FADE OUT) OF SCREENWRITERS

A TURNAROUND OF SCREENPLAYS

A LONG SHOT OF DEVELOPMENT DEALS

A CLOSEUP OF STARS

AN EXTREME CLOSEUP OF SUPERSTARS

A BLACK HOLE OF FADING STARS

A CATTLECALL OF EXTRAS

A WIGGLE OF STARLETS

A GUSH OF FANS

AN ACTION OF FILM DIRECTORS

A TRUCK OF CINEMATOGRAPHERS

A MARK OF SUPPORTING ACTORS

A GRIPE OF GRIPS

A SWOOP OF CRANES

A CUCOLORIS OF GAFFERS

AN AFFLUENCE OF TEAMSTERS

A FLUSH OF HONEYWAGONS

A FACTOR OF MAKEUP ARTISTS

A BREAKDOWN OF PRODUCTION MANAGERS

A MATTE OF SPECIAL EFFECTS

A FOOTPRINT OF FOLEY WALKERS

A CUT OF FILM EDITORS

A FINAL CUT OF FILM PRODUCERS

AN UNKINDEST CUT OF STUDIO PRESIDENTS

A SHUFFLE OF STUDIO EXECUTIVES

AN INGENUITY OF STUDIO ACCOUNTANTS

A CEL OF ANIMATORS

A DEAL OF AGENTS

A RAW DEAL OF AGENTS
When they're not delivering.

A GOOD DEAL OF AGENTS
When they are.

A GREAT DEAL OF AGENTS
Self-explanatory.

A DONE DEAL OF AGENTS
Retired or deceased.

A CACOPHONY OF TV CHANNELS
Caca *for short.*

AN EFFUSION OF TALK SHOW HOSTS

A LAUGHINGSTOCK OF TALK SHOW SIDEKICKS

A VACUITY OF GAME SHOW HOSTS

A FRENZY OF CONTESTANTS

A GLUT OF COMMERCIALS

A LAUGHTRACK OF SITCOMS

A SLAVER OF AWARD SHOWS

A SLO-MO OF SPORTS SHOWS

A DÉJÀ VU OF TV SERIES
Déjà vu *(pronounced* view) *means, of course,* "already seen," *but when mispronounced* déjà vous *(voo), as it is routinely in current English, it means* already you, *which probably isn't what the speaker means. So, the proper, easy* déjà view *is recommended here, everywhere and always.*

A DOLDRUM OF RERUNS

A CHAIN OF ANCHORPERSONS

A BITE OF TV NEWS

Arts & Letters

A MADDER OF PAINTERS

A BLUR OF IMPRESSIONISTS

A BLOCK OF CUBISTS

A BLOT OF ABSTRACT EXPRESSIONISTS

A DECONSTRUCTION OF POST MODERNISTS

A LAYOUT OF MECHANICAL ARTISTS

AN IMPASTO OF LANDSCAPE ARTISTS

A SHOCK OF PERFORMANCE ARTISTS

A WHEEL OF POTTERS

A *VERNISSAGE* OF GALLERIES

A MOLD OF SCULPTORS

A LOLL OF LIFE MODELS

AN IAMB OF POETS

AN ADVANCE OF AUTHORS

A ROYALTY OF BEST-SELLING AUTHORS

AN ENIGMA OF MYSTERY WRITERS

A PRESCIENCE OF SCIENCE-FICTION WRITERS

A BOSOM OF ROMANCE WRITERS
Also, HEAVING BOSOM . . .

A BURROW OF BIOGRAPHERS

A BLIZZARD OF QUOTES

A TEDIUM OF FOOTNOTES

AN APERÇU OF ESSAYISTS

A PROVIDENCE OF PUBLISHERS

A BROWSE OF READERS

One of the points this book hopes to make is that we are virtually surrounded by terms of venery. Even the book you hold in your hand at this moment is a hierarchy of collectives—and I refer not to its content but its structure, beginning with:

A SIGNATURE OF LEAVES
There are sixteen leaves in a signature. Each side of a leaf is one page (which is, of course, why we "leaf" through a book), and two facing pages form

A SPREAD OF PAGES
The signatures are combined in

A GATHERING OF SIGNATURES
This book, and nearly all hard-cover books, are bound in a gathering of signatures. Look at the upper edge of the spine of this book: you will see several "little" books, each bound with its own fine thread. Each of those little books is a signature, and if you count the signatures and multiply by sixteen, you will know the length of the book without opening its cover. But open it anyway.

A GALLEY OF TYPE
A galley is the printer's tray that holds type. Even before a book is bound it is referred to by a collective when the undivided pages are sent out for proofing, and even sometimes review, in galleys.

Religion

AN IMMERSION OF BAPTISTS

A MEMBERSHIP OF PRESBYTERIANS

A GOVERNMENT OF EPISCOPALIANS

A VISIT OF JEHOVAH'S WITNESSES

A BOOK OF MORMONS

A MEETING OF QUAKERS

A GLOSSOLALIA OF PENTECOSTALS

A MASS OF PRIESTS

A FLAP OF NUNS

A SEA OF BISHOPS

A FIDGET OF ALTARBOYS

AN EVENSONG OF CHOIRBOYS

A CALENDAR OF SAINTS

A COMMENTARY OF RABBIS

A KEEN OF CANTORS

A DISPUTATION OF TALMUDISTS

A PILGRIMAGE OF MOSLEMS

AN ULULATION OF MUEZZIN

A FUNDAMENT OF AYATOLLAHS

AN OM OF BUDDHISTS

A TRANSMIGRATION OF HINDUS

A DREADLOCK OF RASTAFARIANS

A DUBIETY OF AGNOSTICS

AN IMPIETY OF ATHEISTS

A SOBRIETY OF CALVINISTS

A PROPRIETY OF AMISH

A PROPHET (*often*, PROFIT) OF TELEVANGELISTS

A CACHE (*often*, CASH) OF GURUS

A HELLFIRE OF FUNDAMENTALISTS

Politics & Law

AN ODIUM OF POLITICIANS

A PODIUM OF ORATORS
AN INFLATION OF DEMOCRATS
A DEFICIT OF REPUBLICANS

A DISAGREEMENT OF STATESMEN

A BRANLE OF DIPLOMATS
A Court dance (appropriate), pronounced "brawl" (very appropriate).

AN EQUALITY OF DISSATISFACTIONS
A genuine Austro-Hungarian political term for an agreement fair to both sides.

A MAZE OF BUREAUCRATS

A BUTTONHOLE OF LOBBYISTS

A COLLECTIVE OF SOCIALISTS

AN EVOLUTION OF COMMUNISTS
Formerly REVOLUTION.

A TWADDLE OF PUBLIC SPEAKERS

A SLUMBER OF THE OLD GUARD

A DRAIN OF THINK TANKS

AN ESCHEAT OF LAWYERS

A SHADOW OF PROCESS-SERVERS

A TRAIL OF SUBPOENAS

A CROSS OF LITIGATORS

A PRESUMPTION OF PROSECUTORS

A PANEL OF JURORS

A DOCKET OF CASES

A DELIVERANCE OF ACQUITTALS
Traditionally, an English clerk demands of the accused, "How do you wish to be tried?" to which the accused replies, "By God and country," prompting the generous "God give you a good deliverance" from the clerk.

A LENGTH OF BRIEFS

AN INSANITY OF CLAUSES

A PITFALL OF FINE PRINT

Journalism

A PAN OF FOOD CRITICS

A PEN OF EDITORIAL CARTOONISTS

A PANEL OF COMIC CARTOONISTS

A SCOOP OF REPORTERS

A PLATITUDE OF SPORTSWRITERS

A PLATITUDE *DU JOUR* OF SYNDICATED COLUMNISTS

A QUERY OF CHECKERS

A MANGLE OF COPY EDITORS

A CAPRICE OF ASSIGNMENT EDITORS

A DYSPEPSIA OF CITY EDITORS

A PENULTIMATUM OF MANAGING EDITORS

AN ULTIMATUM OF EXECUTIVE EDITORS

A PEEK OF GOSSIP COLUMNISTS

A PEAK OF SOCIETY COLUMNISTS

A PIQUE OF POLITICAL COLUMNISTS

A CLICK OF PHOTOGRAPHERS

A CHAPEL OF PRINTERS
A genuine collective, denoting an association of employees in a printing office.

A PIE OF TYPESETTERS

A GOFER OF COPYBOYS

A SHILLING OF NEWSBOYS
In England.

A LABYRINTH OF MAGAZINES
A SLEAZE OF TABLOIDS
A FEEDING FRENZY OF PAPARAZZI
A HYPE OF PRESS AGENTS

Coffee Tobacco
Tin Ware

Business & Finance

A COLUMN OF ACCOUNTANTS

A SIPHON OF TAXES

AN EVAPORATION OF ANNUITIES

A COMMISSION OF BROKERS

A MARGIN OF INVESTORS

A TICK OF BOND SALESMEN

A PROWL OF ARBITRAGEURS

A SIEGE OF INVESTMENT BANKERS

A SEIZURE OF CORPORATE RAIDERS

AN INTEREST OF BORROWERS

A FORECLOSURE OF BANKERS

A CAGE OF TELLERS

A PIGOUT OF SAVINGS AND LOANS

A DRAW OF PARTNERS

A CRISIS OF MIDDLE MANAGERS

A BURNOUT OF VP'S

A GOLDEN PARACHUTE OF CEO'S

AN IMMOLATION OF LBO'S

A TUMULT OF TRADERS

A RECESSION OF ECONOMISTS

A BREAKDOWN OF PLANS

For a term of relatively recent vintage, this expression has achieved wide usage in recent years, and is almost universally applicable today in such expressions as, "The company will shortly issue its latest breakdown of plans."

A HO! HO! OF LOOPHOLES

AN OH! OH! OF AUDITS

A PITCH OF AD AGENCIES

A BITCH OF CLIENTS

A PERSISTENCE OF INSURANCE SALESMEN

A LINE OF TRAVELING SALESMEN

A QWERTY OF TYPISTS

A QWERTY OF BEGINNING TYPISTS

AN OGLE OF OFFICE BOYS

A HASSLE OF HUSTLERS

A PUSH OF PEDDLERS

Travel

A FLARE OF PILOTS
A HOVER OF FLIGHT ATTENDANTS
A STACK OF PLANES
AN ODYSSEY OF LUGGAGE
A GLACIER OF BAGGAGE HANDLERS
AN OVERLOAD OF CONTROLLERS
A RACKET OF HELICOPTERS
A POSTPONEMENT OF TRAINS
A CANCELLATION OF TRAINS
On the surburban lines.
A COMEDY OF AIRLINE SCHEDULES
A TRAGEDY OF RAILROAD SCHEDULES

A TOTEBAG OF PORTERS

A CRAWL OF TRAFFIC

A PARKING LOT OF HIGHWAYS
A BOTTLENECK OF TOLL BOOTHS
AN APATHY OF SERVICE STATIONS
A CRUNCH OF PARKING LOTS
A TRANSPLANT OF MOBILE HOMES

A BASKET OF BALLOONISTS

A SWOOP OF BICYCLES
A SNARL OF MOTORCYCLES
A DRUDGE OF TUGBOATS
A FLAP OF SAILBOATS
A SLAP OF SPEEDBOATS
A GRANDILOQUENCE OF YACHTS
A POSH OF OCEAN LINERS
Perhaps because of its elegant connotation, POSH *has many would-be fathers, none with a preemptive claim. The most interesting theory is that* POSH *is an acronym for "Port Out, Starboard Home," a formula that would assure a stateroom on the cooler northern side of the ship, away from the punishing rays of the tropical sun on the England-India route.*

Cops & Robbers

A COLLAR OF COPS

A FREEZE! OF DETECTIVES
A ROUNDUP OF SUSPECTS
A TRAP OF STATE TROOPERS
A SPECTACLE OF PRIVATE EYES
A SIEVE OF SECURITY SYSTEMS
A SUMMONS OF METER MAIDS
AN EVASION OF SCOFFLAWS

A PERK OF WHITE COLLAR CROOKS

A SCAM OF CON ARTISTS
A SCHEME OF SWINDLERS
A SKIM OF EMBEZZLERS
A HELPING OF PICKPOCKETS
A FACSIMILE OF FORGERS

A KILO OF PUSHERS

A DEMOLITION OF DOPERS

A SEIZURE OF DRUG AGENTS

A LABYRINTH OF MOLES
Espionage variety.

A MAGNUM OF HITMEN

on the heels of
A SPLIT OF SQUEALERS

A BALE OF BONDSMEN

A TRACE OF BOUNTY HUNTERS

AN INFLAMMATION OF ARSONISTS

A CLOACA OF MUGGERS

A COWARDICE OF TERRORISTS
As in cowardice of curs.

AN INNOCENCE OF HOSTAGES

The Armed Services

A MESS OF PRIVATES

A GLOWER OF SERGEANTS

AN INSIGNIFICANCE OF CORPORALS

A BELLOW OF DRILL SERGEANTS
AN INDIGESTION OF MESS SERGEANTS
A GLIMMER OF LIEUTENANTS
A GLAMOUR OF COLONELS
In England: A FOAM OF FLAG OFFICERS, A CONSPIRACY OF CAPTAINS,
A FROWN OF MAJORS, *and* A PURPLE OF GENERALS.

A GLITTER OF GENERALS

A DECK OF SAILORS

A BRIDGE OF ADMIRALS

A WOLFPACK OF SUBMARINES
The Germans' World War II term for their U-boats.

A MUSCLE OF MARINES

A CLANK OF TANKS

A RUMBLE OF ARTILLERY

A SALVO OF SHELLS
On water A BROADSIDE.

A HAILSTORM OF GUNSHIPS

A STORM OF PARATROOPS

A FLUSH OF W. C.'S
Royal Air Force collective for Wing Commanders.

Zoology

AN AARMORY OF AARDVARKS

A BLOAT OF HIPPOPOTAMI

A FLOAT OF CROCODILES

A TOTTER OF GIRAFFES

A STREAK OF TIGERS

A MACHINATION OF MONKEYS

A BUFFOONERY OF ORANGUTANS

A RUMPUS OF BABOONS

A CACKLE OF HYENAS

A PRICKLE OF PORCUPINES

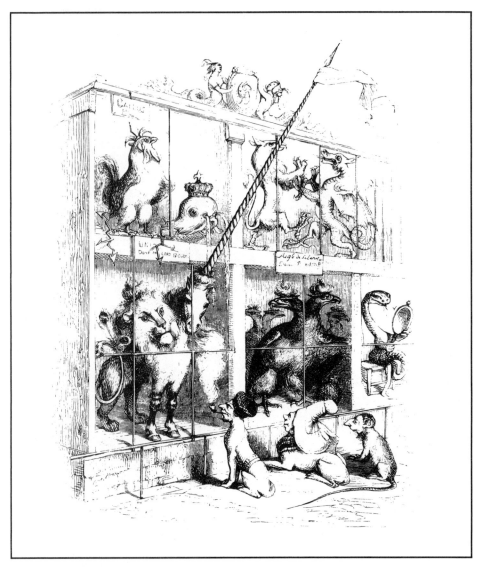

A MARVEL OF UNICORNS

AN IMPLAUSIBILITY OF GNUS

AN IMPROBABILITY OF PUFFINS

AN IMPOSSIBILITY OF PLATYPUSES

AN EXTINCTION OF DODOBIRDS

A QUIVER OF COBRAS

A RHUMBA OF RATTLESNAKES

A WILINESS OF COYOTES

A PROWL OF PUMA

A ROMP OF OTTERS

A MASK OF RACCOONS

A MALOCCLUSION OF BEAVERS

A SCURRY OF SQUIRRELS

A WADDLE OF PEKINGESE

A *MERDE* OF *CANICHES*

A VISE OF PITBULLS

A HOWL OF HOUNDS

A PIDDLE OF PUPPIES

A POUNCE OF CATS

A PEW OF CHURCH MICE

A RUINATION OF RODENTS

A RUMINATION OF COWS

A BATTERY OF RAMS

A CRACKLE OF CRICKETS

A CONFLAGRATION OF FIREFLIES

A VENOM OF SPIDERS

A GULP OF CORMORANTS

A STAND OF FLAMINGO

A SHIMMER OF HUMMINGBIRDS

A SCOLD OF BLUEJAYS

A CHAIN OF BOBOLINKS

A GLISTER OF GOLDFINCHES

A SQUABBLE OF SEAGULLS

A JUBILEE OF EAGLES

A TIME-STEP OF SANDPIPERS

A SWOOP OF SWALLOWS

A WOBBLE OF OSTRICH

A PARADE OF PENGUINS

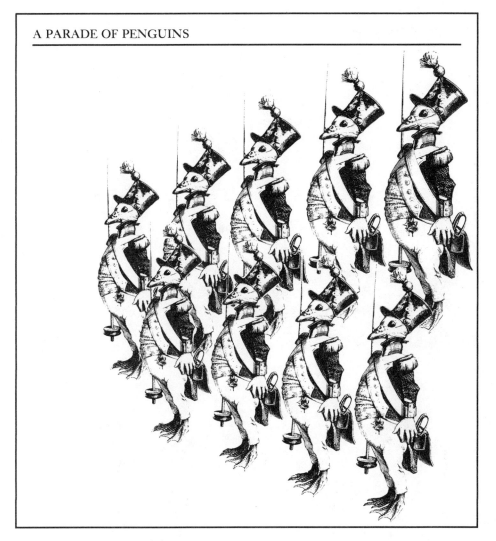

A WAKE OF VULTURES

A CLUTTER OF STARLINGS

A RADIANCE OF CARDINALS

A UBIQUITY OF SPARROWS

A DROPPING OF PIGEONS

A DEATH-ROW OF TURKEYS
in November.

A DRUMMING OF GROUSE

A GATLING OF WOODPECKERS

A PRATTLE OF PARROTS

A DURANTE OF TOUCANS

A KETTLE OF FISH

A FINE KETTLE OF FISH *In the better neighborhoods.*

A GLINT OF GOLDFISH
A SHIVER OF SHARKS
A SCUTTLE OF CRABS
A FLACCIDITY OF CLAMS

Cases in Point

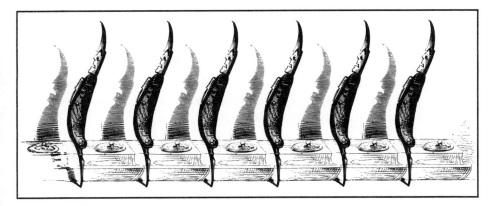

The Comedy of Errors
William Shakespeare
Note how these terms of venery elude us when they become the common coin of our speech. Had it ever occurred to you that *The Comedy of Errors* was a group term, even when I slipped it into the note on DECEIT OF LAPWINGS as a pop quiz? *Is* it a group term? Of course. It can be nothing but. Had Shakespeare called his play "The Avalanche of Errors," the term would have been instantly apparent, but, familiar as he doubtless was with the venereal lists, the poet came up with a more imaginative term. Did he ever do it again? Look below.

A wilderness of monkeys
Shakespeare, *The Merchant of Venice*, Act III, Sc. 1. TUBAL: One of them showed me a ring that he had of your daughter for a monkey. SHYLOCK: Out upon her! Thou torturest me, Tubal. It was my turquoise. I had it of Leah when I was a bachelor. I would not have given it for *a wilderness of monkeys.*

A sea of troubles
Shakespeare, *Hamlet*, Act III, Sc. 1. HAMLET: To be or not to be, that is the question./Whether 'tis nobler in the mind to suffer/The slings and arrows of outrageous fortune,/Or to take arms against *a sea of troubles,*/And by opposing end them . . .

A surfeit of slaughter
Beowulf, c. 1000

A heart of furious fancies
A knight of ghosts and shadows
Tom O' Bedlam, Anon., c. 1530: "With *a heart of furious fancies*/Whereof I am commander . . ./With *a knight of ghosts and shadows*/I summoned am to tourney."

The company of apostles
The fellowship of prophets
The army of martyrs
Te Deum

A cloud of witnesses
Hebrews, 12:1. "Wherefore seeing we also are compassed about with so great *a cloud of witnesses* . . . let us run with patience the race that is set before us."

A rabble of gods
St. Jerome, who, with his contemptuous *turba deorum*, was, of course, denouncing the multiplicity of pagan deities.

A knot of witches
Cotton Mather, *Wonders of the Invisible World*, 1692

A harvest of souls
Alban Butler, *Lives of the Principal Saints*

A grand *democracy* of forest trees
An urgent message for our time from Walt Whitman.

A raft of kings
Mark Twain's Tom Sawyer, in *Tom Sawyer Abroad*, reported "a raft of kings hopping about." See the various notes on *raft*.

A Nest of Gentlefolk
Ivan Turgenev

A Diversity of Creatures
Rudyard Kipling

A coven of kettles
Dylan Thomas, *Under Milk Wood*

A springul of larks
Dylan Thomas, *Poem in October*

Screams of newsboys
James Joyce, *Ulysses*

An amazement of women
Lawrence Durrell, *Monsieur*

A crocodile of choirboys
Evelyn Waugh, *Brideshead Revisited*

A cloud of bats
A crowd of walruses
A battery of quills
Life Natural History: The Mammals

A scavenging of gulls
Thomas Pynchon, *Gravity's Rainbow*

A press of ghosts
Iris Murdoch, *The Book and the Brotherhood*

"S. J. Perelman: A Basket of Grovels"
Wilfrid Sheed, *Essays in Disguise*

A squalor of honest men
Stephen Crane, 1899, in an epigraph: "A newspaper is a court/Where
every one is kindly and unfairly tried/By *a squalor of honest men*."

A prisonhouse of nations
V. I. Lenin, quoting Herzen on the Russian Empire under the Czars.

A drizzle of empires
In November, 1918, Winston Churchill described Central Europe as
"*a drizzle of empires* falling slowly through the air."

A bodyguard of lies
During the Second World War, Churchill justified disinformation with
the description, "truth attended by *a bodyguard of lies*."

A marathon of deletions
Art critic Harold Rosenberg on the work of Rauschenberg, Warhol
and Newman.

An abyss of playwrights
John Simon, *New York Magazine*

"A gaggle of newspaper columnists came, as did a phalanx of figures
from the publishing industry."
The New York Times account of Malcolm Forbes' funeral, March 2, 1990.

Afterword

A CLUTCH OF SECOND THOUGHTS
As usual, the French have a rather nice word for it: l'esprit de l'escalier, the thought on the stairway *that we* should *have uttered in company but didn't think of until we were on our way out—or home in bed—and it was too late to dazzle anyone but ourselves.*

A FLIGHT OF YESTERDAYS

A TWINKLING OF TODAYS

A PROMISE OF TOMORROWS

The
Game of Venery
Second Move

Inventi la partita!, invent the game, the Italians say. Very well. It's high time. In the twenty-two years of its existence, *An Exaltation of Larks* has become, spontaneously, a game, with rules and sides and winners and losers. I should have known it would, since I'm the one who has called it a game from the beginning—because, as you've probably guessed by now, it was a game before it was a book, a game I thought I had invented (until I discovered Dame Juliana's 1486 version), and played (relentlessly) with my friends and fellow writers. One day in 1968 I decided that the only way to organize the heap of venereal terms scrawled over the years, on envelopes, menus, matchbook covers, boxtops and scraps of paper was to write a book. That is how *An Exaltation of Larks* was born.

The first edition of *An Exaltation of Larks* contained, as does this one, a Tom Sawyerly invitation to the reader to take a brush from the bucket and help me paint the fence, and, beyond my wildest expectations, thousands of readers have. They have also, extempore, reinvented the game. Letters from every continent have recounted riotous venereal evenings (subspecies linguistic) of improvised play. The Ultimate Edition seeks to impose order on this festive chaos.

Again, an acknowledgement is in order to the legion of players of the Game of Venery, but especially to Maggie and Jerome Minskoff, David and Leslie Newman, George Plimpton, Edward Tivnan, Marilyn Bethany, Dr. David Pearce and Gerry Cooney, who served as guinea pigs, and agile players, in the practice scrimmages of the Game as it was developed for these pages.

The First Move in the Game of Venery was mine, the Second is yours.

VENEREAL SOLITAIRE

Not at all what it sounds like, this innocent game can be played alone, using the Index at the end of the book, which, as you can see, has been designed both to direct the reader to any term in the book, and to permit the reader to fill in his or her own terms for any or all of the more than 1,100 nouns in the Index. A pencil is suggested, with an eraser, so the game can be played more than once.

Double Solitaire can be played by two players, alternating turns and reading their terms aloud. Solitaire isn't scored; the invention is the reward.

All the remaining games are scored. As these games evolved and I debated the wisdom of creating a zero-sum game, in which there must always be a winner and loser, I recalled the occasion when critic Clive Barnes was invited to a New York Knicks basketball game with the inducement, "It's just like ballet," and Barnes replied, "Good. I'll come when they don't keep score." Barnes's logic is persuasive, but in the end I have yielded to the competitive spirit that has animated the *ad hoc* players of the game.

GROUP GAMES

Since these are Games of Venery, and we know that venery refers to the hunt, each variation of the Game is a *Chase*, played by *Hunters* and presided over by a *Master of the Chase* who is one of the Hunters. The Master of the Chase chooses the Chase that will be played ("dealer's choice"), and judges the terms that are invented. At the end of the Chase, a new Master takes over (by any practical system of rotation), chooses the next Chase (it may be the same Chase or any variation), and judges the terms. Since the judging of the Game is necessarily subjective, the rotation of the position of Master assures balance in the judging (Show bias against others and they will show bias against you).

The details of the Game will be described in the context of the Chases, but in general:

Each player is a **Hunter**.

Each game is a **Chase**.

All the Chases together comprise a **Hunt**.

Before each chase, the Hunters rotate as **Master of the Chase**.

In each Chase, the Master **chooses the Chase** and the **Time Limit, judges the terms** and awards **Hits**.

At the end of the Chase, the highest number of **Hits** wins the Chase, and is awarded a **Juliana**.

At the end of the Hunt, the highest numbers of **Julianas** wins the game.

The only tools needed are pads of paper, writing implements and an inquiring mind.

Chase I

If it is the first chase of the Hunt, the Master is chosen arbitrarily or by lot. The Master selects a Chase. If Chase I is chosen, here is how it is played.

The Chase Master picks five Categories from the Table of Contents: for example, Professions, High Life, Low Life, Sports and Arts & Letters. *The Categories needn't be limited to the twenty-five in this book* (though I hope you will find them comprehensive).

When the Master has announced the five Categories, each Hunter catches (creates and writes down) **one full term** (that is, *term* and *noun*) for each of the five categories, for example, A SLEW OF KILLERS for the Low Life Category, AN UPPITY OF SNOBS for the High Life Category, etc. Obviously, they needn't be terms from the book; it's better if they're not. *Care should be taken by each player not to reveal his or her catches until the time is up.*

TIME LIMIT: Before the Chase begins, a time limit is set by the Master of the Chase (the Hunters may consult): anything from two minutes for experts or Hunters in a hurry, to five minutes for a more leisurely Chase.

When the time is up, the Master calls the first Category, and each Hunter reads his term for that Category. When all the terms for a Category have been read, the Master of the Chase selects the best one by awarding **a Hit** (a point) which the Hunter stows, figuratively, in his or her game bag, thus keeping track of the Hits, which will be totaled at the end of the Chase to determine the winner. *The Master may elect to award no Hits in a Category (if no term is deemed worthy of a Hit), or, where two terms are of equal merit, a Hit to each of the two (but never more than two) winning Hunters.*

Though the judging system may seem arbitrary, and subject to bias and even manipulation, you will find that, as the terms are read, there is usually loud consensus on the best term, and occasionally even louder—and perhaps more enjoyable—disagreement. But isn't that how the Game—and the language—grow?

When the terms for all five Categories have been read, **each Hunter's Hits are totalled** and the winner (or each winner in the event of an equality of accumulated Hits) is awarded **a Juliana** (for Dame Juliana, the patron saint of the Game of Venery), which is stowed in the winner's game bag.

At that point all game bags are empty, except for the Juliana. Hits do not accumulate from Chase to Chase, Julianas do.

With the winner of the first Chase determined, the role of Master of the Chase rotates (to the left around the room, for example), and the new Master selects the next Chase, which may be the same one or another.

Chase II

The time limit is set, and **the Master selects five** nouns. They may be from the book, or of the Master's invention; for example, RATS, RACING CARS, COMEDIANS, ROLLS ROYCES and MAIDEN AUNTS. Within the time limit, each Hunter must catch a *term* for each of the *nouns*, for example, A RIMSHOT OF COMEDIANS, A SNARL OF RACING CARS, etc.

When the time is up and the terms are read aloud, in turn, by their creators, The Master awards a Hit for the best *term* for each of the *nouns*, all the Rat terms being read first and a Hit awarded, then the Racing Car terms, etc.. The Hunters keep a record of their Hits in their game bags.

When all the Hits have been awarded, the Hunter with the greatest number wins that Chase, and records the Juliana in his or her game bag.

The game bags are now empty of Hits for the next Chase, and the role of Master rotates.

Chase III

The time limit is set, and **the Master selects five** *terms*. They may be from the book, or five inventions by the Master, for example, A RUSH, A CRUSH, AN UGLINESS, A PENANCE, A BLISS. Now, within the time limit, each Hunter much attach a *noun* to each *term*, for example, A RUSH OF FRATER-NITIES, A CRUSH OF SCHOOLGIRLS, etc.

When time is up, each Hunter reads his or her term of venery for RUSH, and a Hit is awarded; then the newly invented term of venery for CRUSH is judged, etc. When the Master has awarded a Hit (or none, or two in the event of a draw) for the best *noun* for each of the *terms*, the Hunter with the greatest number of Hits wins this Chase, and stows the Juliana in his or her game bag. *Remember: the Julianas are cumulative from Chase to Chase, the Hits are not.*

Game bags are emptied of all but Julianas, and the role of Master rotates.

Chase IV

A variation of Chases I, II and III, Chase IV is a speed game. The Master decides whether the Chase will consist of Categories, *nouns* or *terms*; then, if, for example, there are six Hunters (not counting the Master of the Chase), the Master writes six Categories (if that is his choice), or six *nouns* or *terms* on *separate* slips of paper, one item to a piece of paper, *the number of slips always equaling the number of Hunters.*

The slips are put into a bowl and drawn, *one slip to a player.* Each person has one minute to catch a term of venery by completing the slip: a *noun* if the slips have *terms*, a *term* if the slips have *nouns*, a full term of venery if the slips have Categories.

The terms are then read aloud and the Master selects a winner. Since this is a speed game, requiring only a minute to play, and each person catches only one term, there are no Hits given: the winner gets a Juliana for his or her game bag.

Chase V

In this variation on Chase IV, *each Hunter* writes on a slip of paper one Category, or one *noun*, or one *term*, depending on which of the three options the Master has chosen. The options are never mixed (it would complicate judging): all the slips contain Categories—or *nouns*—or *terms*.

The slips are folded, *signed*, and given to the Master, who distributes them, making sure no Hunter gets his or her own slip.

Each Hunter has one minute to catch a venereal term and complete the slip. Then, the slips are read (six players, six slips; seven players, seven slips), and the Master awards a Juliana to the winner (like Chase IV, this is a speed game and doesn't award Hits).

TEAM GAMES

Chase VI

As always, one Hunter is Master of the Chase. The remaining Hunters are divided into **two Packs (teams) of equal size**.

The Master selects a Category from the book, or invents one.

Within a one-minute time limit, each Hunter writes a *noun* of that Category on a slip of paper (AIRLINERS, BOTTLES, OTTERS, etc.). The slips of Pack A are collected and given to the Master, as are the slips of Pack B. The Master distributes (randomly) Pack A's *nouns* to Pack B, and vice versa, one slip to a Hunter.

The clock is restarted and each Hunter has two minutes (or any agreed-upon time limit) to catch a proper *term* for the *noun* he or she has drawn. For example, the Hunter who has wound up with OTTERS, may add A ROMP OF.

Pack A, Hunter 1 reads his or her completed term of venery; Pack B, Hunter 1 reads his or hers. The Master awards a Hit (or none, or two in the case of a draw). The process is repeated with Hunters 2 on each side, then Hunters 3, etc., until all the Hunters have been paired off against each other, with the Master rendering a verdict *for each pair*.

When all the pairs have been pitted against each other, the Hits are totted up, and *one of the teams* is awarded a Juliana, which it stows in its game bag.

The Master is rotated.

Chase VII

Chase VII is a variation on Chase VI, the only difference being that the teams exchange *terms*, and fill them out with *nouns*.

*

As you see, a Hunt can consist of any number of Chases, in any combination or order, and the Chases can be played by individuals or teams. In the course of a Hunt, individual Chases may be played to determine one winner, and/or team Chases may be played to find a winning team. The variations, while not infinite, are manifold.

To review: the players are Hunters, one of them designated Master of the Chase, on a rotating basis. Each game is a Chase. In some Chases the Master awards Hits, a record of which is kept in the Hunter's metaphorical game bag, to be totaled to determine the winner of a Chase, who is awarded a Juliana. Each time the winner of a Chase is declared, all game bags are empty—*except for the Julianas, which are cumulative.* **When the Hunt ends, the holder of the most Julianas is the game's winner.**

In the team games, the Pack collects Julianas in its game bag, and at the end of the Hunt, **the team with the greater number of Julianas wins.**

I have proposed seven Chases: the history of *An Exaltation of Larks* augurs many more. I wish you happy hunting (the nice thing about this hunt is that nothing dies but the occasional ego), and, in farewell, have one request: if you come up with an especially zesty game, share it with the rest of us . . .

. . . and it goes without saying, if you catch a splendid term of venery—*and you will*—let me know. But I didn't have to say that, did I.

Index

Explicit
James Lipton
in
An Exaltation of Larks

FOR THE BEST IN PAPERBACKS, LOOK FOR THE

In every corner of the world, on every subject under the sun, Penguin represents quality and variety—the very best in publishing today.

For complete information about books available from Penguin—including Penguin Classics, Penguin Compass, and Puffins—and how to order them, write to us at the appropriate address below. Please note that for copyright reasons the selection of books varies from country to country.

In the United States: Please write to *Penguin Group (USA), P.O. Box 12289 Dept. B, Newark, New Jersey 07101-5289* or call 1-800-788-6262.

In the United Kingdom: Please write to *Dept. EP, Penguin Books Ltd, Bath Road, Harmondsworth, West Drayton, Middlesex UB7 0DA.*

In Canada: Please write to *Penguin Books Canada Ltd, 90 Eglinton Avenue East, Suite 700, Toronto, Ontario M4P 2Y3.*

In Australia: Please write to *Penguin Books Australia Ltd, P.O. Box 257, Ringwood, Victoria 3134.*

In New Zealand: Please write to *Penguin Books (NZ) Ltd, Private Bag 102902, North Shore Mail Centre, Auckland 10.*

In India: Please write to *Penguin Books India Pvt Ltd, 11 Panchsheel Shopping Centre, Panchsheel Park, New Delhi 110 017.*

In the Netherlands: Please write to *Penguin Books Netherlands bv, Postbus 3507, NL-1001 AH Amsterdam.*

In Germany: Please write to *Penguin Books Deutschland GmbH, Metzlerstrasse 26, 60594 Frankfurt am Main.*

In Spain: Please write to *Penguin Books S. A., Bravo Murillo 19, 1° B, 28015 Madrid.*

In Italy: Please write to *Penguin Italia s.r.l., Via Benedetto Croce 2, 20094 Corsico, Milano.*

In France: Please write to *Penguin France, Le Carré Wilson, 62 rue Benjamin Baillaud, 31500 Toulouse.*

In Japan: Please write to *Penguin Books Japan Ltd, Kaneko Building, 2-3-25 Koraku, Bunkyo-Ku, Tokyo 112.*

In South Africa: Please write to *Penguin Books South Africa (Pty) Ltd, Private Bag X14, Parkview, 2122 Johannesburg.*